BOX-MAKING
PROJECTS *for the*
Scroll Saw

BOX-MAKING PROJECTS *for the Scroll Saw*

BY GARY MACKAY

Fox Chapel Publishing

1970 Broad Street • East Petersburg, PA 17520
www.FoxChapelPublishing.com

Acknowledgments

Thanks to the following people who have encouraged and inspired me to write this book:

My wife, Helen, whose suggestions and photography were constantly appreciated.

My book editor, Gretchen Bacon, Peg Couch, and the staff at Fox Chapel Publishing Company.

Friends and customers who have kept me busy working on my scroll saw.

Alan Giagnocavo
Publisher

Peg Couch
Acquisition Editor

Gretchen Bacon
Editor

Troy Thorne
Book Design

Linda Eberly
Layout

Greg Heisey
Cover & Project Photography

Box-Making Projects for the Scroll Saw is an original work, first published in 2006 by Fox Chapel Publishing Company, Inc. The patterns contained herein are copyrighted by the author. Readers may make three copies of these patterns for personal use. The patterns themselves, however, are not to be duplicated for resale or distribution under any circumstances. Any such copying is a violation of copyright law.

ISBN-13: 978–1–56523–294–5
ISBN-10: 1–56523–294–1

Publisher's Cataloging-in-Publication Data

MacKay, Gary.

 Box-making projects for the scroll saw / Gary MacKay. -- East Petersburg, PA : Fox Chapel Publishing, 2006.

 p. ; cm.

 ISBN-13: 978-1-56523-294-5
 ISBN-10: 1-56523-294-1
 Includes index.

 1. Wooden boxes. 2. Woodwork--Patterns. 3. Woodworking tools. 4. Jig saws. I. Title.

TT180 .M33 2006
684/.08--dc22   0609

To learn more about the other great books from Fox Chapel Publishing, or to find a retailer near you, call toll-free 1-800-457-9112 or visit us at *www.FoxChapelPublishing.com.*

Note to Authors: We are always looking for talented authors to write new books in our area of woodworking, design, and related crafts. Please send a brief letter describing your idea to Peg Couch, Acquisition Editor, 1970 Broad Street, East Petersburg, PA 17520.

Printed in China
10 9 8 7 6 5 4 3 2 1

About the Author

Gary MacKay is a designer and box maker who lives with his wife, Helen, in Myrtle Beach, South Carolina. He has been designing, making, and selling boxes in craft galleries for more than 20 years.

Gary first started woodworking during his high school years when he used a jigsaw to make an end table from pine. After buying a band saw in 1985, he sold band saw boxes through consignment shops in northern Vermont. Now, he concentrates on designing and making wooden items that can be cut on a scroll saw. He is currently juried through the South Carolina Artisans Center, one of the craft galleries where his work is on display.

Gary likes to use his scrap wood to make snowflake ornaments and intarsia projects. Whenever he is not working in his woodshop, he can be found out on the golf course or in the vegetable garden. Gary is a frequent contributor to *Scroll Saw Woodworking & Crafts* magazine. This is his first book for Fox Chapel Publishing.

CONTENTS

INTRODUCTION

The purpose of this book is to show woodworkers several scroll sawing techniques that can be used to make boxes on the scroll saw. We'll look at several different types of boxes including boxes with lids, drawers, contrasting woods, wooden hinges, box joints, ring trays, pierced earring holders, and compartment dividers.

The first chapter focuses on boxes with lids, an ideal starting point because these are the easiest boxes to make. Next are boxes with drawers, which were designed to show how easy it is to use stacked layers for box making, and laminated boxes, which include some simple techniques for laminating contrasting woods. Boxes that use box joints follow, and this chapter includes some great techniques for creating box joints on the scroll saw. Finally, we'll take a look at the different types of compartments you can make to customize the perfect jewelry box. In each chapter, you'll find a complete step-by-step demonstration followed by patterns for additional projects. A Quick Cuts box is included for each project to provide you with a quick reference to the general steps necessary to create each part of each box. The Quick Cuts steps are grouped by part rather than by the step-by-step order, so you'll want to refer back to the step-by-step demonstration for additional information.

Though some of the techniques may be slightly more difficult than others, all of the boxes in this book are deceptively simple. Each box may look like it took hours and a complex pattern to complete, but, actually, the boxes are made using simple patterns and techniques. Many of the boxes use a scroll sawing technique called stack cutting. The great thing about stack cutting wood on a scroll saw is that you do not need to follow the pattern lines precisely. Stack-cut pieces of wood will fit perfectly to their adjacent pieces of wood. By stack cutting laminated wood, you can produce boxes with checkerboard, diamond, pinwheel, and pie-piece-shaped designs—just about any shape you can think of. The end result is a beautiful box that looks like it took hours upon hours to create.

While each type of box teaches different skills, they are also designed to be decorative and useful. My main passion is designing and making jewelry boxes, projects that serve both form and function. The ones in this book feature three unique designs: ring trays, pierced earring holders, and dividers. I have also included several other boxes with practical uses: The opened lid of the *Recipe Box* holds the recipe while you cook. The *Paper Clip Box, Pencil and Pen Box,* and *Notepad Box* will keep your desk organized. Each project is designed to show off your woodworking skills by creating a beautiful, yet functional, end product.

I hope that you enjoy making the boxes in this book and that you will use some of the techniques presented to create other scrolling projects.

—Gary MacKay

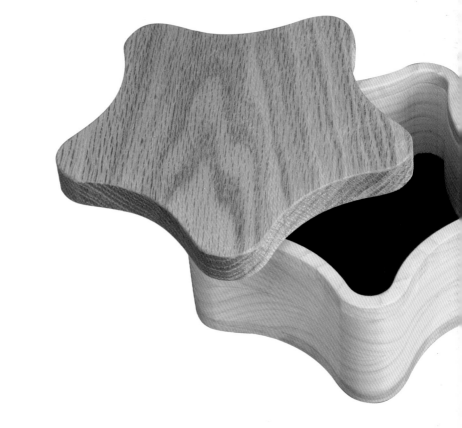

Box-Making Basics

Making boxes is a rather simple prospect—once you understand a few basic principles. In this chapter, we'll explore the basic elements of box making. You'll learn about the types of wood recommended for these projects, the tools you'll need to make them, and tips to adding some finishing touches.

Wood

I used 11 different wood species to make the boxes featured in this book. Some of the woods were ones that I've used many times before, like cherry, poplar, and walnut; others, like alder and sassafras, I used for the first time.

"Machine-ability," or how a wood cuts on the scroll saw, is the most important factor in choosing wood for your boxes. For example, red oak and maple are more difficult to cut on a scroll saw than some of the other woods. If you are new to using a scroll saw, you'll want to start with wood that is softer than red oak and maple.

In addition to the degree of difficulty in cutting the wood, you'll also want to consider its color. By using contrasting woods to create the patterns, you will make your boxes really stand out.

The finished look of the wood is another consideration when you are choosing wood. All of the boxes in this book are given a natural, or clear, finish to show off the grain of the wood.

A fancy jewelry box is an ideal candidate for a highly figured and beautifully colored wood like cherry or walnut. A heart-shaped keepsake box for a small child would be best made out of a durable wood like red oak. If you plan to paint your box, you'll want to choose an inexpensive wood that will sand very smooth, like basswood or poplar.

One final consideration is cost. I used some of the more expensive woods, like cherry, mahogany, and walnut, on the thinner front and back pieces for some of the boxes in this book. Using these woods in limited areas helped to cut down on the cost of the woods but still gave the boxes a high-class, expensive look.

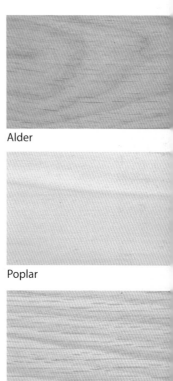

Alder

Poplar

Red Oak

Walnut

You'll want to consider machine-ability, color, grain pattern, and cost when choosing wood for your boxes. Shown here are four of the woods used in this book—alder, poplar, red oak, and walnut.

WOOD COMPARISON CHART

Wood	Color	Machine-ability	Cost	Characteristics
Alder	Reddish brown	Easy	Moderate	Nice grain, resembles cherry
Ash	Light golden brown	Medium	Low	Nice grain, resembles oak
Basswood	Light tan	Easy	Low	Nice grain, resembles poplar
Butternut	Golden brown	Medium	Moderate	Beautiful grain, resembles white walnut
Cherry	Reddish	Medium	High	Beautiful grain, resembles alder
Mahogany	Reddish brown	Medium	High	Beautiful grain, resembles cherry
Maple	Light reddish brown	Hard	Moderate	Nice grain, resembles basswood
Poplar	Light yellowish tint	Easy	Low	Nice grain, resembles basswood
Red oak	Golden brown	Hard	Medium	Nice grain, resembles ash
Sassafras	Pale to dark brown	Medium	Low	Unique smell, nice grain, resembles ash
Walnut Dark	Brown to black	Medium	High	Beautiful grain, great contrasting wood

In addition to a scroll saw, box making requires several types of clamps, a simple jig, a few varieties of adhesives, and some common household items.

TOOLS

You don't need a lot of tools to make boxes on a scroll saw. In fact, in addition to a scroll saw, all you will need are some clamps, a simple jig, and a few different types of adhesives.

SCROLL SAW AND BLADES

You can use any scroll saw to make boxes. I recommend that your scroll saw have a dust blower to keep the pattern lines free of dust. A light

with a magnifier will help you see the pattern lines when you are cutting. You do not need a scroll saw with a speed control or quick-change blade clamps to make boxes because all of the boxes in this book can be cut on one speed and do not require frequent blade changes.

For cutting boxes on your scroll saw, I recommend the following blades:

- #5 reverse-tooth blade for woods ¼" to ½" thick
- #7 reverse-tooth blade for woods ¾" thick
- #12 reverse-tooth or thick-wood blade for woods greater than ¾" thick

OTHER TOOLS

Of the other tools that are useful in box making, clamps are some of the most important. At a minimum, it is a good idea to have two screw-type clamps, two quick-grip clamps, and several 2" spring clamps.

A band saw with a ¼"-wide blade is an optional tool that can be used on some boxes to cut the outside profile. (The same cuts can be made with a scroll saw; however, they will be more difficult. Use a #12 reverse tooth or a thick-wood scroll saw blade and proceed slowly.)

Another optional but handy tool is the stationary belt sander. I recommend this tool because of its ease and speed of use. You can get the same results, however, with a handheld power sander or with several grits of sandpaper wrapped around a wood block or dowel and some elbow grease.

JIGS

When making boxes, it is very handy to have a simple jig made from wood that you can use as a flat, square surface for gluing up wood. In this book, a gluing jig will be used for gluing laminations, box lids, and boxes. The jig allows you to clamp the wood together to create a tight wood joint (see the sidebar, "Making a Gluing Jig," at the right).

Always protect the surface and rails of your gluing jig from glue squeeze-out with a single sheet of old newspaper as shown in the top right photo.

GLUES, ADHESIVES, AND TAPES

Glues, adhesives, and tapes are important materials in box making. Don't try to omit their use from your project. The few minutes it takes to add packaging tape over a pattern or to position and reposition glued, clamped wood will pay off in the end with a nicer finished project.

Wood glue: I use wood glue for all of the boxes I make. I always place a single sheet of old newspaper on a flat surface when gluing pieces of wood together. Be sure to check for glue squeeze-out and remove it with a flathead, or slotted, screwdriver or a rag.

When gluing two pieces of wood together, apply glue to both mating surfaces. With glue, as soon as you apply pressure on the first clamp, the mating surfaces will slide out of position. You may need to unclamp and reposition your pieces several times before they stay in the position you want.

A simple gluing jig gives you a flat, square surface for gluing up wood.

MAKING A GLUING JIG

TOOLS AND MATERIALS

◆ Wood glue
◆ Square
◆ 1 to 2 screw clamps

STOCK

◆ One piece ¾" x 18" x 24" pressboard, MDF (medium-density fiberboard), or plywood
◆ One piece ¾" x ¾" x 17" oak rail
◆ One piece ¾" x ¾" x 22¼" oak rail
◆ Three pieces ½" x ¾" x 3¾" scrap wood clamping blocks

Glue the two rails to the piece of ¾" x 18" x 24" pressboard, MDF, or plywood that is used for the base at 1" from the base edges. Use a square to ensure a 90-degree angle.

1

Don't apply too much clamping pressure to a glue joint or you will force all of the glue out of the joint. Apply just enough pressure to produce a small amount of glue squeeze-out.

Spray adhesive or glue stick adhesive: Use spray adhesive on larger patterns and glue stick adhesive on smaller patterns. I have found that you need to adhere the pattern to your workpiece just before you do your cutting. Some patterns adhered overnight become loose with time.

Packaging tape: Cover your patterns with clear packaging tape after the patterns are applied to the wood. The packaging tape serves as a blade lubricant. The tape can be applied before the pattern if light glare is a problem.

Double-sided tape: I like to use several thin strips of double-sided tape when adhering two pieces of wood together prior to stack cutting for making laminations. When using double-sided tape, separate the release paper using a pin.

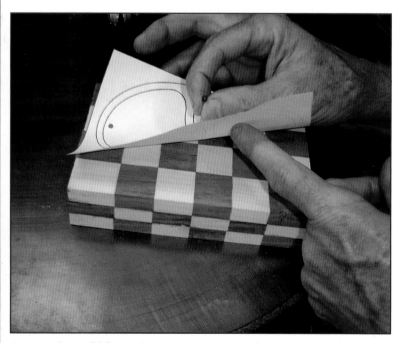

A pin can be useful for centering a pattern, especially on laminated stock.

TECHNIQUES

Two special scroll sawing techniques are used to make the boxes in this book. These techniques are also common woodworking practices, but they have been altered so they can be done on a scroll saw. One is stack cutting; the other is laminating. I also use a technique called precision pinpoint pattern placement to center patterns perfectly on the stock.

STACK CUTTING

Stack cutting is simply placing two or more pieces of wood together to cut the same pattern. The result of this technique is that you will have several pieces of the same shape. Stack cutting is a time-saver if you need to cut multiple pieces. You can cut the same kinds of wood or different kinds in a single stack. By cutting two different kinds of wood, you can also ensure a perfect fit when you are cutting a pattern like the pinwheel box.

LAMINATING

Laminating involves gluing two or more pieces of wood together before a pattern is scrolled. One reason to laminate a board is to get a thicker or wider piece for scrolling. Another reason to laminate wood is to create a pattern. By gluing together different types of wood and cutting the laminated piece into strips, you can create checkerboard and diamond patterns.

PRECISION PINPOINT PATTERN PLACEMENT

A pin can be used to accurately center a pattern on your workpiece. This is what I call "precision pinpoint pattern placement." First, mark the center of your workpiece. Next, apply spray adhesive to your pattern. Then, stick a pin through the center of the pattern and slide the pattern all the way up to the head of the pin. Now, stick the point of the pin in the center of your workpiece and slide the pattern down the pin. Finally, press the pattern into place and remove the pin. Your pattern is perfectly placed.

FINISHING

All of the boxes in this book have been finished with a natural finish. I prefer a natural finish to paint or stain because it allows the natural beauty of the wood to show through. Many hardwoods have beautiful grain patterns and lovely colors for box making.

To finish a box, I first sand the entire box to 220 grit or finer. Many finishes have been ruined by dried glue spots, so I like to apply a light coat of paint thinner after I finish sanding to detect any dried glue spots on the box. I use a pencil to circle any areas of dried glue. Once the thinner evaporates, I sand off the pencil circles.

My first coat of finish is boiled linseed oil (tung oil or Danish oil are two other choices) applied with a rag, as it really brings out the wood grain. After the box has dried for two days, I use a 1" brush to apply a coat of clear shellac. When the shellac has dried, I sand the box with 320-grit sandpaper, and then apply a good paste wax to the box.

LINING BOXES WITH FELT

Lining box compartments of all shapes with felt is easy. Here is the "no bake" recipe.

You will need wood glue, poster board, and felt. Place a sheet of newspaper on a flat surface, apply wood glue to the poster board, and roll the felt evenly onto the poster board. Cover the felt with a piece of newspaper, and place some heavy books or magazines on top. Leave it overnight to dry. Use a pencil to mark the size of the compartment you are lining on the poster board. Cut out the lining with sharp scissors.

Place a few drops of tacky glue on the poster board prior to inserting the lining into the compartment. Sheets of felt that have been glued to poster board tend to curl, particularly

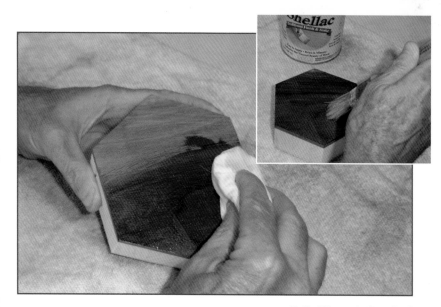

if it is humid. Gluing the felt-covered poster board directly to the wood of the compartment will prevent this tendency.

If you will be lining an odd-shaped compartment, like a heart shape, be sure to save the cutout from the compartment with the pattern still adhered. Place the cutout pattern-side down on the poster board, and trace the shape on the poster board with a pencil.

Boiled linseed oil applied as a first coat really brings out the grain. A coat of shellac, applied after the linseed oil is dry, helps protect the box.

SAFETY

Staying safe is key to enjoying your craft. Remember the following as you are working:

- Use safety goggles to protect your eyes.
- Remove any loose clothing or jewelry.
- Work in a well-ventilated area, and use a mask or an air cleaner to protect your lungs.
- Work in a well-lighted area.
- Keep your hands away from the blade.
- Don't use a scroll saw when you are tired or unfocused.

Backing felt with poster board makes it easier to line your box compartments.

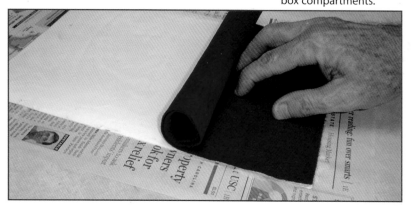

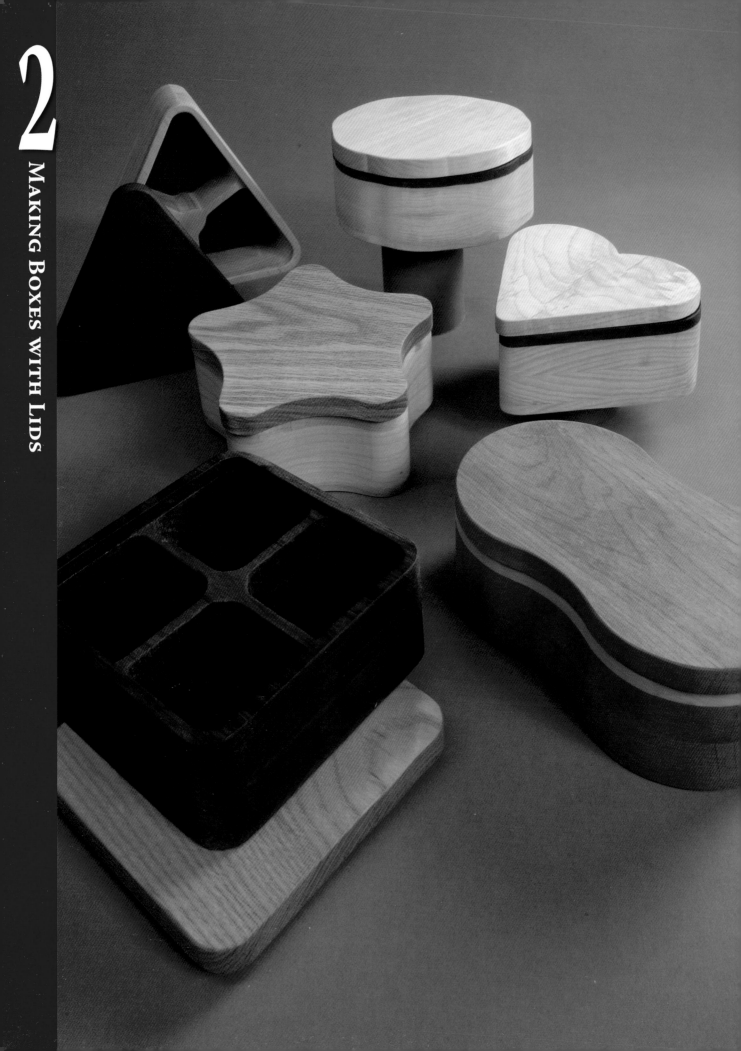

MAKING BOXES WITH LIDS

These boxes are easy to make on your scroll saw. Any combination of woods can be used to add contrast to the lid, the lid liner, or the box. The box compartments can easily be lined in felt or in velvet.

All of the boxes in this chapter can be made using ¼", ½", and ¾" surfaced wood. The following pages take you through the steps in making the *Square Box*. The same technique is used to make all of the boxes in this chapter.

SQUARE BOX

This box is an easy shape to make on a scroll saw. The walnut box with an ash lid makes a nice contrasting-woods box.

TOOLS AND MATERIALS

◆ One photocopy each of the lid, box, and lid liner patterns
◆ Temporary bond spray adhesive
◆ Thick-wood or #12 reverse-tooth blade for cutting the box
◆ #5 reverse-tooth blade for cutting the lid and the lid liner
◆ Drill or drill press and ⅛" and 1⁄16"drill bits
◆ Clear packaging tape
◆ Sandpaper, 80, 150, and 220 grit
◆ Wood glue
◆ Clamps
◆ Masking tape
◆ Screwdriver
◆ Felt or velvet (optional, for lining)
◆ Finish of choice

STOCK

◆ Two pieces of ¾" x 5½" x 5½" for box
◆ One piece of ½" x 5½" x 5½" for lid
◆ Two pieces of ¼" x 5½" x 5½" for lid liner and box bottom

Overall size:
5" long x 5" wide x 2½" high
Wood: Ash and walnut

SQUARE BOX

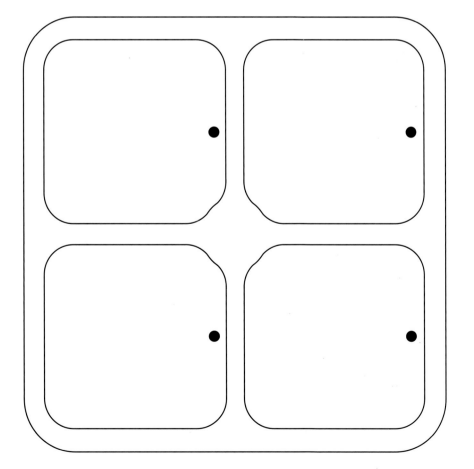

Lid pattern

Make one photocopy of the lid pattern.

Enlarge pattern 110%

Box pattern

Make one photocopy of the box pattern.

Pattern dots indicate blade entry holes.

Enlarge pattern 110%

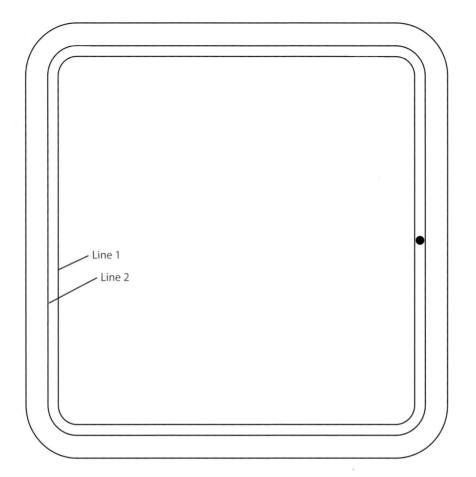

Line 1

Line 2

Lid liner pattern

Make one photocopy of the lid liner pattern.

Pattern dot indicates blade entry hole.

Enlarge pattern 110%

QUICK CUTS

BOX

◆ Glue two pieces of wood for box together.
◆ Apply box pattern to stock.
◆ Drill ⅛" blade entry holes as indicated on pattern.
◆ Cut four compartments from box.
◆ Sand wood fuzzies off box bottom.
◆ Glue one ¼" x 5½" x 5½" piece of wood on bottom of box.
◆ Glue outside lid liner to top of box.
◆ Cut outside profile of box.

LID

◆ Apply pattern to stock.
◆ Cut around the pattern line for lid.

LID LINER

◆ Apply pattern to stock.
◆ Drill 1⁄16" blade entry hole where indicated on pattern.
◆ Cut around Line 2.
◆ Cut around Line 1.
◆ Glue outside lid liner to top of box.
◆ Glue inside lid liner to lid.

1

Glue and clamp the two ¾" x 5½" x 5½" pieces of wood together for the box. Let the glue dry according to the manufacturer's directions.

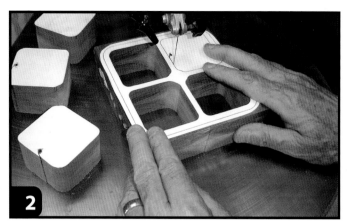

2

Adhere the box pattern to the now 1½" x 5½" x 5½" box piece of wood. Then, cover the pattern with clear tape. Drill four ⅛" blade entry holes, and cut out the four compartments. Save one waste piece from the cut-out compartment if you plan to line your box. Do not remove the patterns.

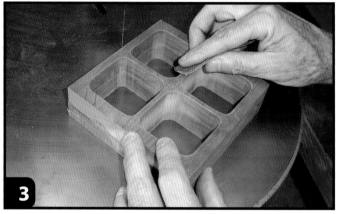

3

Use a piece of folded 150-grit sandpaper to sand the wood fuzzies from the bottom of the box.

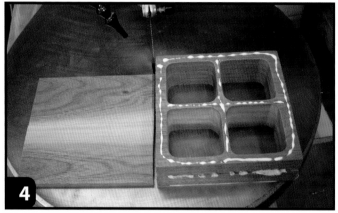

4

Put a light layer of glue on the bottom of the box. Then, place one ¼" x 5½" x 5½" piece of wood for the box bottom on the glued surface.

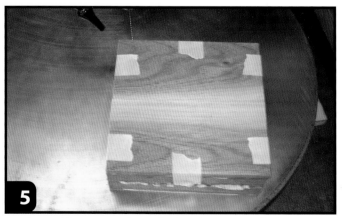

5

Apply masking tape to keep the box bottom in place.

6

Clamp the box bottom to the box. Use a screwdriver to remove glue squeeze-out, and then let the glue dry.

7

Apply the lid pattern to the ½" x 5½" x 5½" lid stock. Cover it with clear packaging tape. Then, cut the outside pattern line for the lid using a #5 reverse-tooth blade.

8

Remove the lid pattern.

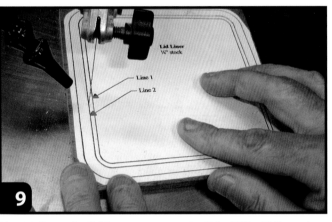

9

Now, adhere the lid liner pattern to the ¼" x 5½" x 5½" stock for the lid liner. Drill a ¹⁄₁₆" blade entry hole where indicated on the pattern. Then, cut around Line 2 on the pattern. This will create the outside lid liner. Do not remove the pattern.

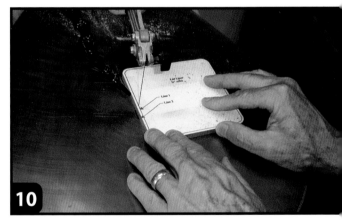

10

Cut around Line 1. Now you have the inside lid liner.

11

Remove the pattern from the top of the box.

12

Glue the outside lid liner to the top of the box. Use masking tape to hold the lid liner onto the top of the box. The outside lid liner will seat the lid and inside lid liner correctly above the compartments.

13

Clamp the box for five minutes.

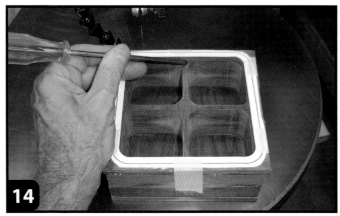

14

Unclamp the box and remove glue squeeze-out with a screwdriver. Then, reclamp the box and let the glue dry.

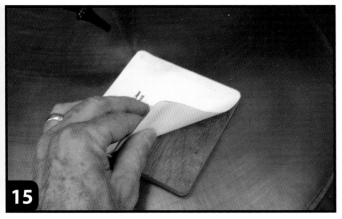

15

Remove the pattern from the inside lid liner.

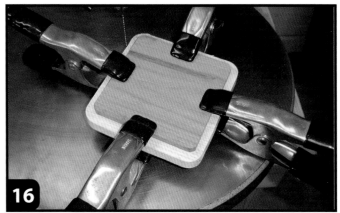

16

Put glue on one surface of the inside lid liner. Center it on the lid. Then, clamp the inside lid liner and lid together. Let the glue dry.

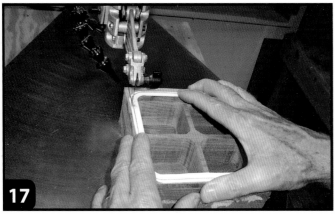

17

Cut the outside profile of the box around the pattern line.

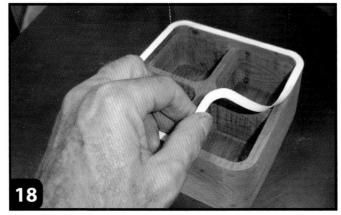

18

Now that all of the cutting is complete, remove the outside lid liner pattern. Sand the entire box through 220 grit. Then, apply the finish of your choice. You can also choose to line the compartments with felt or velvet. (For more information on finishing techniques, see the Finishing section on page 5.)

TRIANGLE BOX

This box is an unusually shaped box that has plenty of room for small items. The poplar box is easy to cut, and the walnut lid makes a nice contrast to the poplar box.

Overall size: 6" long x 6" wide x 2½" high
Wood: Poplar and walnut

TOOLS AND MATERIALS

- One photocopy each of the lid, box, and lid liner patterns
- Temporary bond spray adhesive
- Thick-wood or #12 reverse-tooth blade for cutting the box
- #5 reverse-tooth blade for cutting the lid and the lid liner
- Drill or drill press and ⅛" and ¹⁄₁₆"drill bits
- Clear packaging tape
- Sandpaper, 80, 150, and 220 grit
- Wood glue
- Clamps
- Masking tape
- Screwdriver
- Felt or velvet (optional, for lining)
- Finish of choice

STOCK

- Two pieces ¾" x 5½" x 6¼" for box
- One piece ½" x 5½" x 6¼" for lid
- Two pieces ¼" x 5½" x 6¼" for lid liner and box bottom

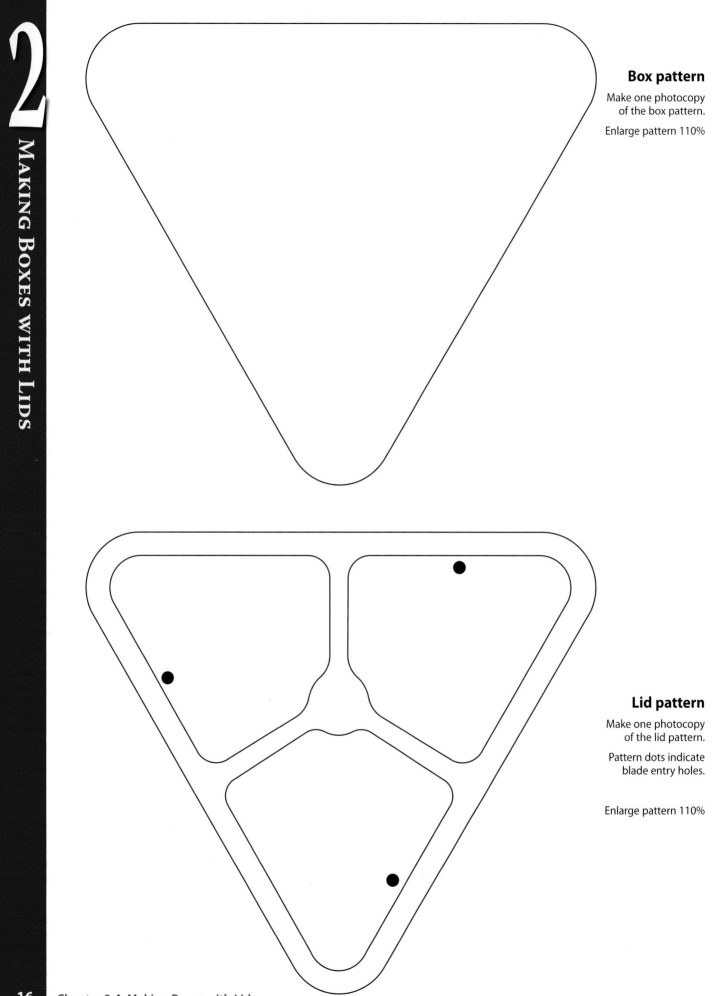

Box pattern

Make one photocopy of the box pattern.

Enlarge pattern 110%

Lid pattern

Make one photocopy of the lid pattern.

Pattern dots indicate blade entry holes.

Enlarge pattern 110%

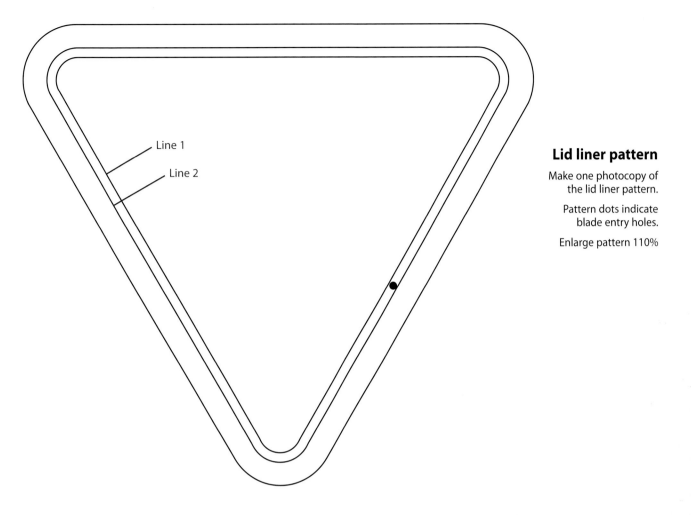

Line 1

Line 2

Lid liner pattern

Make one photocopy of the lid liner pattern.

Pattern dots indicate blade entry holes.

Enlarge pattern 110%

QUICK CUTS

BOX

- Glue two pieces of wood for box together.
- Apply box pattern to stock.
- Drill ⅛" blade entry holes as indicated on pattern.
- Cut out three compartments from box.
- Sand wood fuzzies off box bottom.
- Glue one ¼" x 5½" x 6¼" piece of wood to bottom of box.
- Glue outside lid liner to top of box.
- Cut outside profile of box.

LID

- Apply pattern to stock.
- Cut around the pattern line for lid.

LID LINER

- Apply pattern to stock.
- Drill ¹⁄₁₆" blade entry hole where indicated on pattern.
- Cut around Line 2.
- Cut around Line 1.
- Glue outside lid liner to top of box.
- Glue inside lid liner to lid.

STAR BOX

Adding rounded corners to a typical star shape gives this box some additional room. I used poplar for the box and red oak for the lid. Maple was used for the lid liner.

Overall size: 5¾" long x 5¾" wide x 2½" high
Wood: Maple, oak, and poplar

TOOLS AND MATERIALS

◆ One photocopy each of the lid, box, and lid liner patterns
◆ Temporary bond spray adhesive
◆ Thick-wood or #12 reverse-tooth blade for cutting the box
◆ #5 reverse-tooth blade for cutting the lid and the lid liner
◆ Drill or drill press and ⅛" and 1⁄16" drill bits
◆ Clear packaging tape
◆ Sandpaper, 80, 150, and 220 grit
◆ Wood glue
◆ Clamps
◆ Masking tape
◆ Screwdriver
◆ Felt or velvet (optional, for lining)
◆ Finish of choice

STOCK

◆ Two pieces ¾" x 6" x 6" for box
◆ One piece ½" x 6" x 6" for lid
◆ Two pieces ¼" x 6" x 6" for lid liner and box bottom

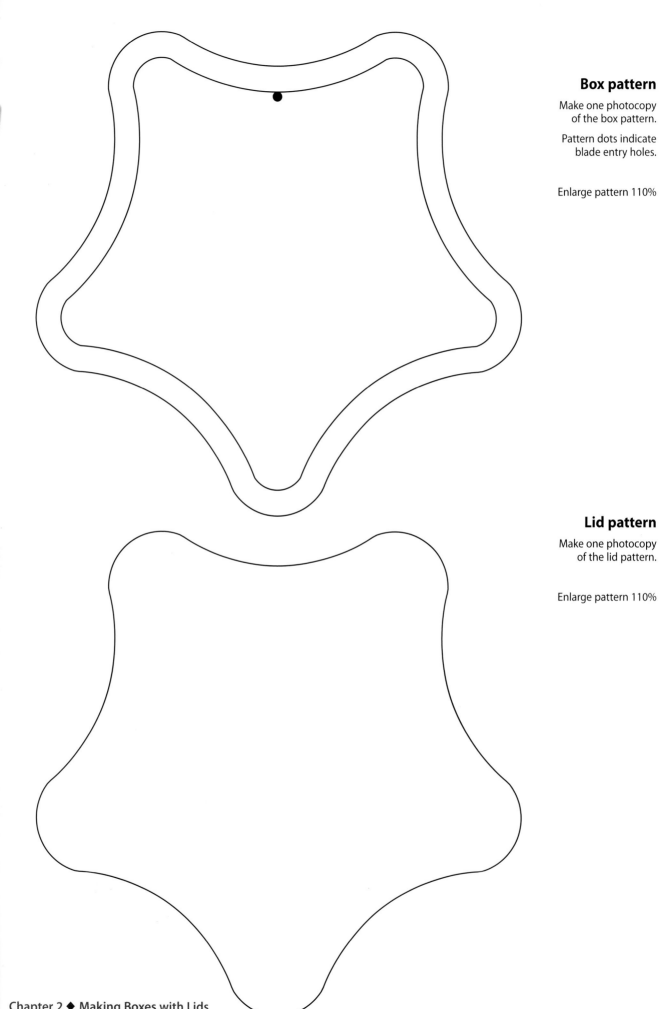

Box pattern

Make one photocopy of the box pattern.

Pattern dots indicate blade entry holes.

Enlarge pattern 110%

Lid pattern

Make one photocopy of the lid pattern.

Enlarge pattern 110%

STAR BOX

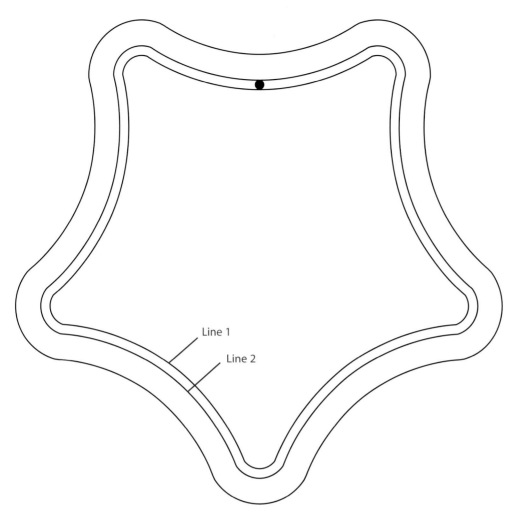

Line 1
Line 2

Lid liner pattern

Make one photocopy of the lid liner pattern.

Pattern dots indicate blade entry holes.

Enlarge pattern 110%

QUICK CUTS

BOX

- ◆ Glue two pieces of wood for box together.
- ◆ Apply box pattern to stock.
- ◆ Drill ⅛" blade entry holes as indicated on pattern.
- ◆ Sand wood fuzzies off box bottom.
- ◆ Glue one ¼" x 6" x 6" piece of wood to bottom of box.
- ◆ Glue outside lid liner to top of box.
- ◆ Cut outside profile of box.

LID

- ◆ Apply pattern to stock.
- ◆ Cut around the pattern line for lid.

LID LINER

- ◆ Apply pattern to stock.
- ◆ Drill ¹⁄₁₆" blade entry hole where indicated on pattern.
- ◆ Cut around Line 2.
- ◆ Cut around Line 1.
- ◆ Glue outside lid liner to top of box.
- ◆ Glue inside lid liner to lid.

HEART BOX

This heart-shaped box makes a great Valentine's Day or birthday gift to show someone what you can make on a scroll saw. The heart box is made from poplar, and the lid is made from a piece of maple with a beautiful grain pattern. Walnut was used for the lid liner.

Overall size: 5¼" long x 4¾" wide x 2½" high
Wood: Maple, poplar, and walnut

TOOLS AND MATERIALS

◆ One photocopy each of the lid, box, and lid liner patterns

◆ Temporary bond spray adhesive

◆ Thick-wood or #12 reverse-tooth blade for cutting the box

◆ #5 reverse-tooth blade for cutting the lid and the lid liner

◆ Drill or drill press and ⅛" and 1⁄16"drill bits

◆ Clear packaging tape

◆ Sandpaper, 80, 150, and 220 grit

◆ Wood glue

◆ Clamps

◆ Masking tape

◆ Screwdriver

◆ Felt or velvet (optional, for lining)

◆ Finish of choice

STOCK

◆ Two pieces ¾" x 5" x 5½" for box

◆ One piece ½" x 5" x 5½" for lid

◆ Two pieces ¼" x 5" x 5½" for lid liner and box bottom

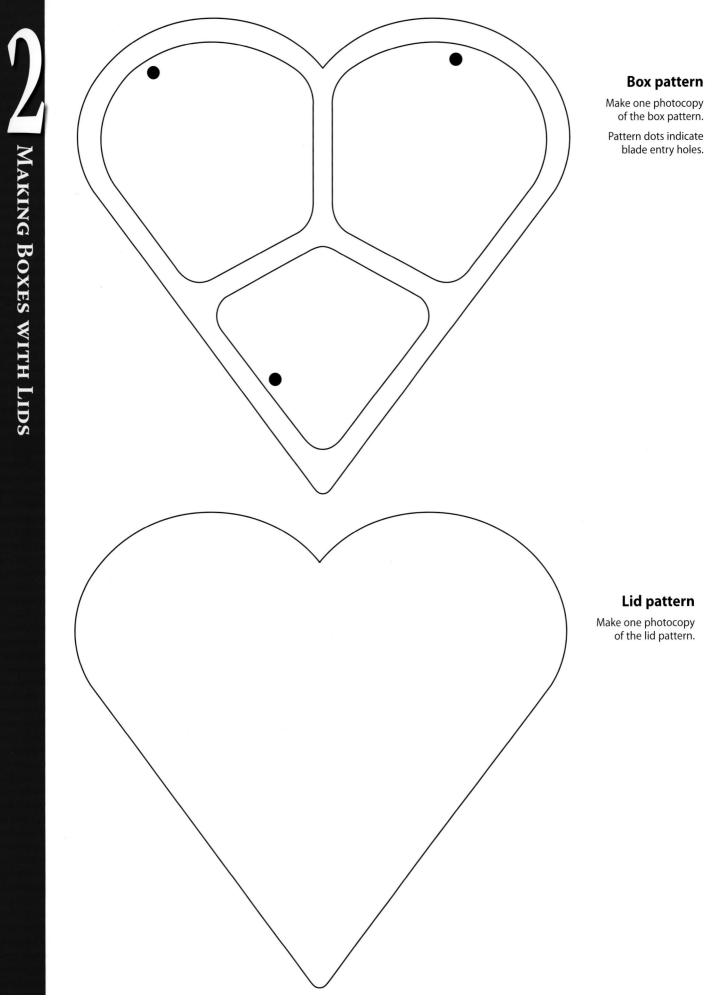

Box pattern

Make one photocopy
of the box pattern.

Pattern dots indicate
blade entry holes.

Lid pattern

Make one photocopy
of the lid pattern.

HEART BOX

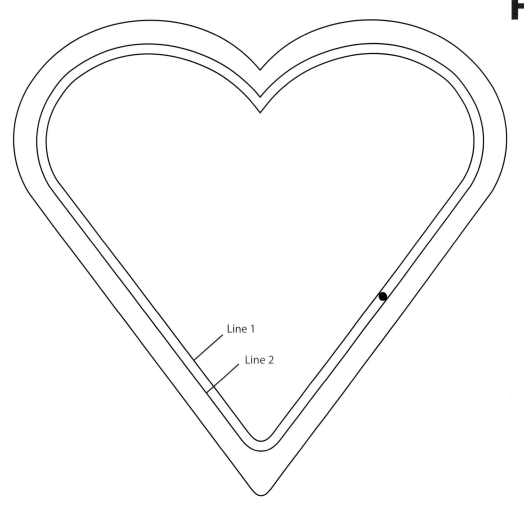

Line 1

Line 2

QUICK CUTS

BOX

◆ Glue two pieces of wood for box together.

◆ Apply box pattern to stock.

◆ Drill ⅛" blade entry holes as indicated on pattern.

◆ Cut out three box compartments.

◆ Sand wood fuzzies off box bottom.

◆ Glue one ¼" x 5" x 5½" piece of wood to bottom of box.

◆ Glue outside lid liner to top of box.

◆ Cut outside profile of box.

LID

◆ Apply pattern to stock.

◆ Cut around the pattern line for lid.

LID LINER

◆ Apply pattern to stock.

◆ Drill 1⁄16" blade entry hole where indicated on pattern.

◆ Cut around Line 2.

◆ Cut around Line 1.

◆ Glue outside lid liner to top of box.

◆ Glue inside lid liner to lid.

PEANUT BOX

This box has a unique shape and shows that you can have differently shaped compartments. The box is made from alder, which looks and machines just like cherry. The lid is also made from alder; the lid liner is poplar.

Overall size: 7" long x 4" wide x 2½" high

Wood: Alder and poplar

TOOLS AND MATERIALS

- One photocopy each of the lid, box, and lid liner patterns
- Temporary bond spray adhesive
- Thick-wood or #12 reverse-tooth blade for cutting the box
- #5 reverse-tooth blade for cutting the lid and the lid liner
- Drill or drill press and ⅛" and ¹⁄₁₆" drill bits
- Drill bit for blade entry holes (for #5 reverse-tooth blade)
- Clear packaging tape
- Sandpaper, 80, 150, and 220 grit
- Wood glue
- Clamps
- Masking tape
- Screwdriver
- Felt or velvet (optional, for lining)
- Finish of choice

STOCK

- Two pieces ¾" x 4½" x 7½" for box
- One piece ½" x 4½" x 7½" for lid
- Two pieces ¼" x 4½" x 7½" for lid liner and box bottom

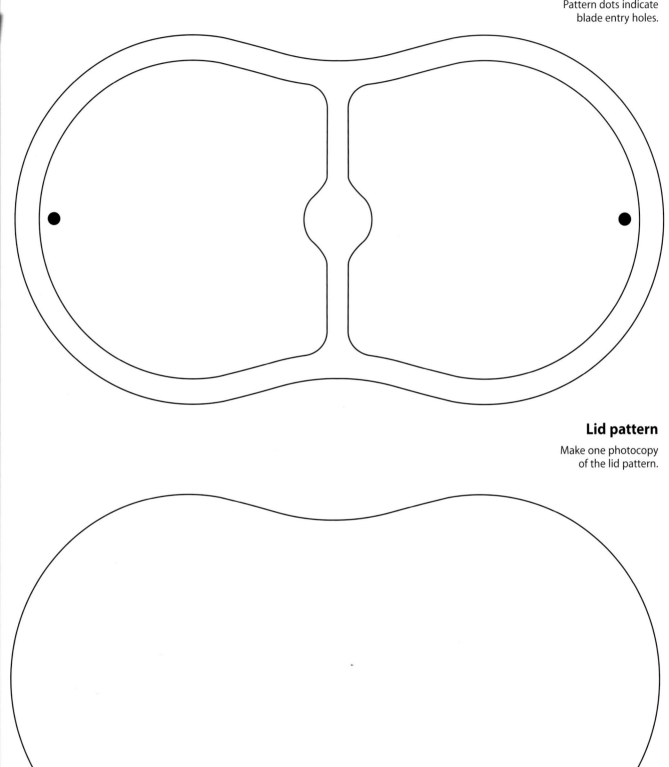

Box pattern

Make one photocopy
of the box pattern.

Pattern dots indicate
blade entry holes.

Lid pattern

Make one photocopy
of the lid pattern.

PEANUT BOX

Lid liner pattern

Make one photocopy
of the lid liner pattern.

Pattern dots indicate
blade entry holes.

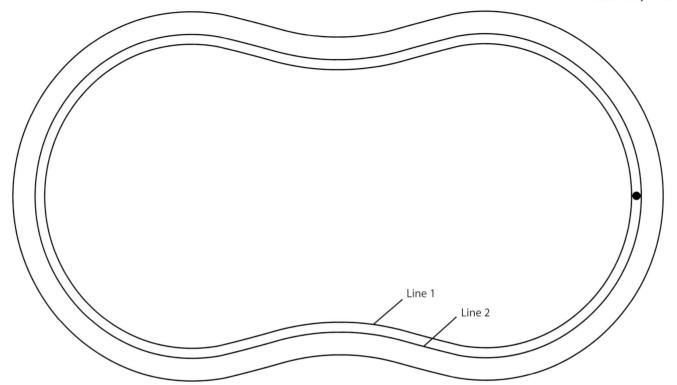

Line 1

Line 2

QUICK CUTS

BOX

- Glue two pieces of wood for box together.
- Apply box pattern to stock.
- Drill ⅛" blade entry holes as indicated on pattern.
- Cut out two compartments from box.
- Sand wood fuzzies off box bottom.
- Glue one ¼" x 4½" x 7½" piece of wood onto bottom of box.
- Glue outside lid liner to top of box.
- Cut outside profile of box.

LID

- Apply pattern to stock.
- Cut around the pattern line for lid.

LID LINER

- Apply pattern to stock.
- Drill ¹⁄₁₆" blade entry hole where indicated on pattern.
- Cut around Line 2.
- Cut around Line 1.
- Glue outside lid liner to top of box.
- Glue inside lid liner to lid.

SEWING BOX

The sewing box's shape allows for the storing of all the small sewing or knitting items that are needed. I scrolled the box and lid from poplar and added a contrasting lid liner of walnut.

Overall size: 5¾" long x 5¾" wide x 2½" high
Wood: Poplar and walnut

TOOLS AND MATERIALS

◆ One photocopy each of the lid, box, and lid liner patterns
◆ Temporary bond spray adhesive
◆ Thick-wood or #12 reverse-tooth blade for cutting the box
◆ #5 reverse-tooth blade for cutting the lid and the lid liner
◆ Drill or drill press and ⅛" and 1⁄16"drill bits
◆ Clear packaging tape
◆ Sandpaper, 80, 150, and 220 grit
◆ Wood glue
◆ Clamps
◆ Masking tape
◆ Screwdriver
◆ Felt or velvet (optional, for lining)
◆ Finish of choice

STOCK

◆ Two pieces ¾" x 6" x 6" for box
◆ One piece ½" x 6" x 6" for lid
◆ Two pieces ¼" x 6" x 6" for lid liner and box bottom

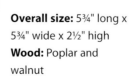

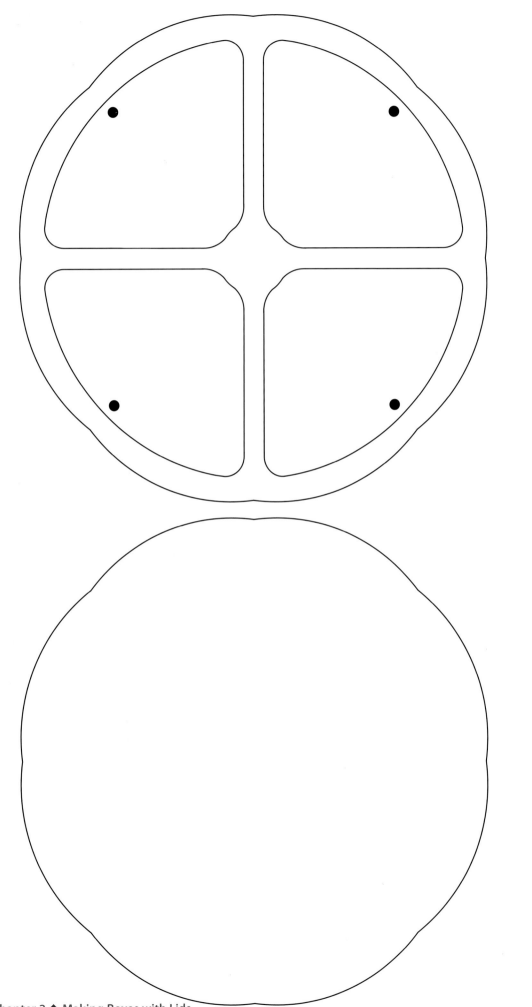

Box pattern

Make one photocopy of the box pattern.

Pattern dots indicate blade entry holes.

Enlarge pattern 110%

Lid pattern

Make one photocopy of the lid pattern.

Enlarge pattern 110%

SEWING BOX

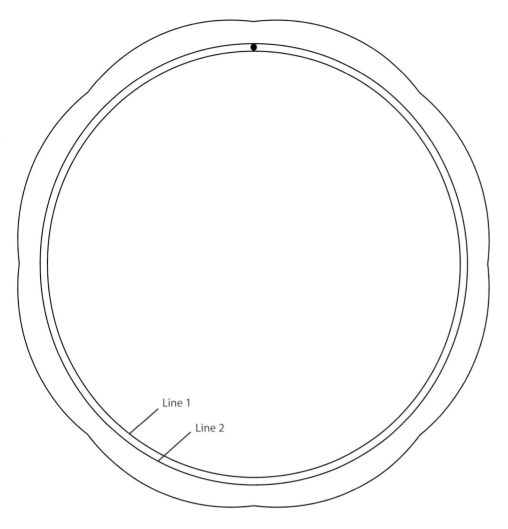

Line 1

Line 2

Lid liner pattern

Make one photocopy of the lid liner pattern.

Pattern dots indicate blade entry holes.

Enlarge pattern 110%

QUICK CUTS

BOX

- Glue two pieces of wood for box together.
- Apply box pattern to stock.
- Drill ⅛" blade entry holes as indicated on pattern.
- Cut out four compartments from box.
- Sand wood fuzzies off box bottom.
- Glue one ¼" x 6" x 6" piece of wood to bottom of box.
- Glue outside lid liner to top of box.
- Cut outside profile of box.

LID

- Apply pattern to stock.
- Cut around pattern line for lid.

LID LINER

- Apply pattern to stock.
- Drill ¹⁄₁₆" blade entry hole where indicated on pattern.
- Cut around Line 2.
- Cut around Line 1.
- Glue outside lid liner to top of box.
- Glue inside lid liner to lid.

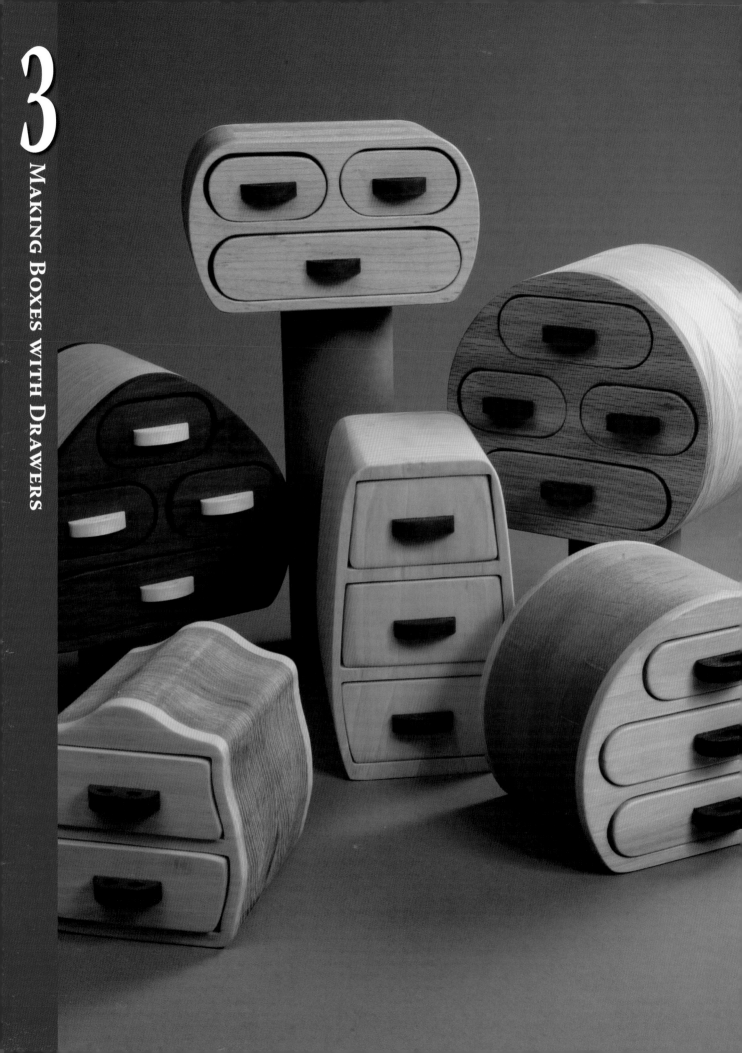

MAKING BOXES WITH DRAWERS

When you first see these boxes with drawers, you may wonder how boxes this large can be made on a scroll saw. These boxes are made by cutting out drawer openings on four ¾" pieces of wood, gluing the four pieces back together, and gluing on box and drawer fronts and backs.

All of the boxes in this chapter can be made from ¼", ½", and ¾" surfaced wood. These boxes really stand out when you use woods of contrasting colors. More expensive woods can be used on the fronts and backs of the boxes and on the drawer fronts and backs since this wood is only ¼" thick. You can select drawer pulls from one of the patterns and easily scroll out drawer pulls for your box. As a finishing touch, line the drawers with felt or velvet.

The following pages take you through the steps for making the *Peaked-Top Box*, which has four drawers. All of the boxes in this chapter are made using the same techniques.

PEAKED-TOP BOX

This box, having four drawers, makes a uniquely shaped box for storing small items. I made the box from poplar and used the more expensive walnut as a contrast for the front and back of the box. The drawer pulls were made from poplar.

Overall size: 5¾" long x 5" high x 3½" deep
Wood: Poplar and walnut

TOOLS AND MATERIALS

- Six photocopies of the box pattern
- Temporary bond spray adhesive
- #9 reverse-tooth blade for cutting ¾"-thick stock and box profile
- #5 reverse-tooth blade for cutting ¼"- and ½"-thick stock
- ¹⁄₁₆" drill bit
- Clear packaging tape
- Mineral spirits
- Sandpaper, 80, 150, and 220 grit
- Drum sander or sandpaper wrapped around wooden dowel
- Wood glue
- Clamps and scrap wood blocks
- Rag, to wipe away excess glue
- Masking tape
- Screwdriver
- Double-sided tape
- Felt or velvet (optional, for lining)
- Finish of choice

STOCK

- Four pieces ¾" x 5¼" x 6" for box and drawers
- One piece ½" x 5¼" x 6" for drawers
- Three pieces ¼" x 5¼" x 6" for drawer fronts and backs and box front and back
- One piece ¼" x ¾" x 6" for drawer pulls

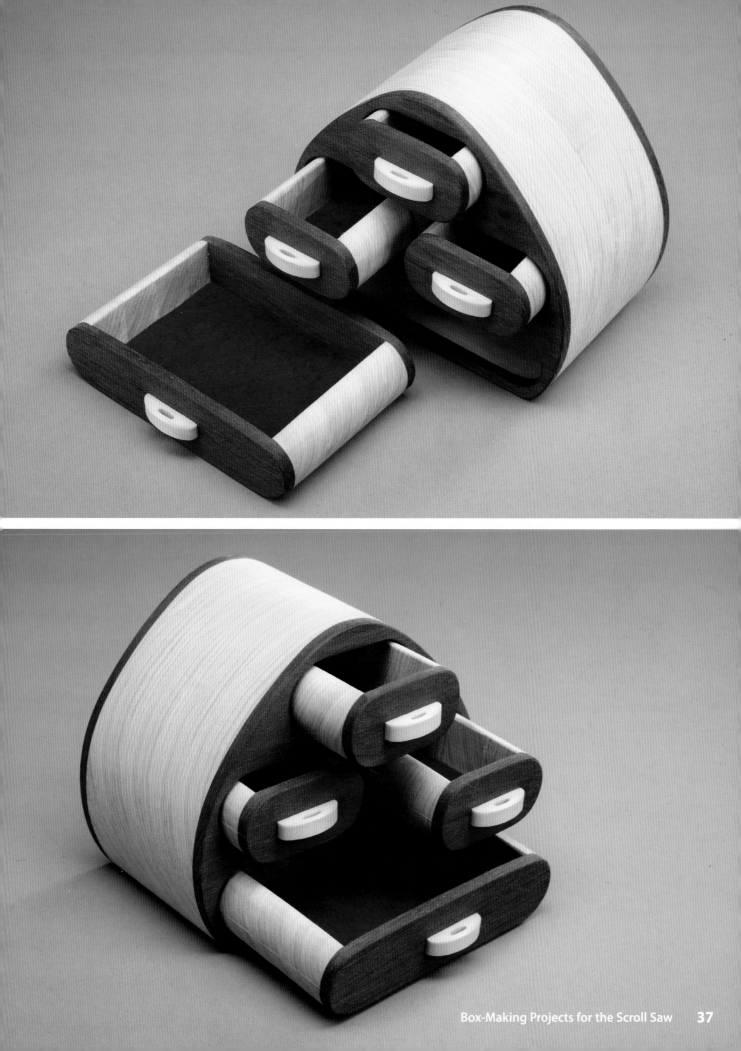

Box patter...

Make six photocop...
of the box patte...

Pattern dots indica...
blade entry hol...

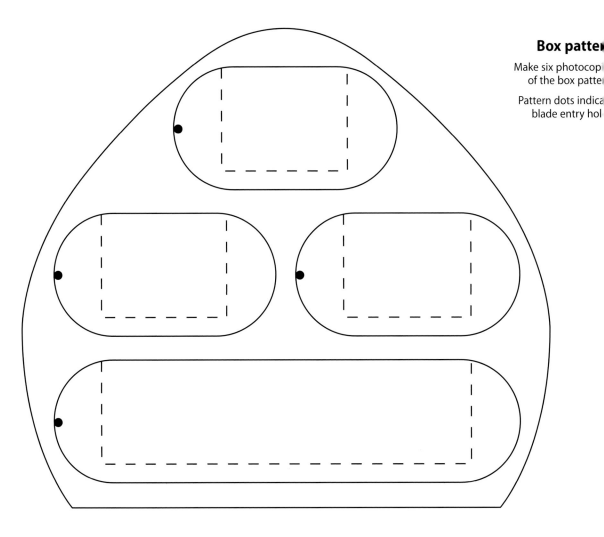

QUICK CUTS

BOX

- Cut out drawers and outside profile from four ¾" pieces of wood.
- Glue four box pieces together.
- Cut out drawers on ½" piece of wood.
- For each drawer, cut out three ¾" drawer compartments and one ½" drawer compartment, following dashed pattern lines.
- Glue each drawer together using three ¾" pieces and one ½" piece of wood.
- Using three ¼" pieces of wood, cut out box front and back and all drawer fronts and backs.

- Select drawer pull pattern and cut out required number of drawer pulls.
- Glue drawer pulls to drawer fronts.

DRAWER PULLS

- Apply pattern to stock for number of drawer pulls needed.
- Tilt scroll saw table 10 degrees, right side down.
- Cut out drawer pulls, following cut direction arrows.

DRAWER PULLS

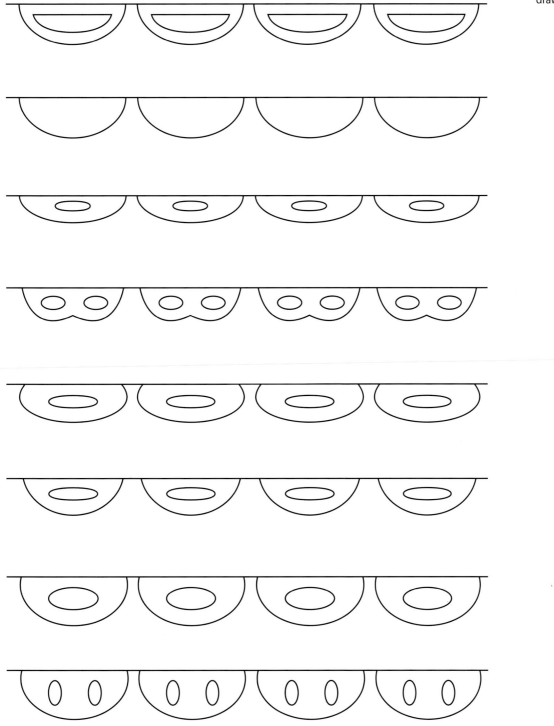

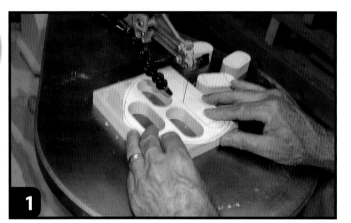

1 Adhere a box pattern to each of the four pieces of ¾" x 5¼" x 6" stock. Cut out all drawers, following the solid pattern lines. Do not cut on the dashed lines yet.

2 Cut the outside profile on all four pieces.

3 Remove patterns from each of the four box pieces. Use mineral spirits to remove stubborn sections of the pattern. Do not remove patterns from the four drawer cutouts.

4 Use a piece of folded 150-grit sandpaper to remove the wood fuzzies from the box pieces.

5 Make sure that the former blade entry holes are lined up. In this case, all of the former holes are on the left-hand side.

6 Apply a thin layer of glue to both surfaces of two box pieces.

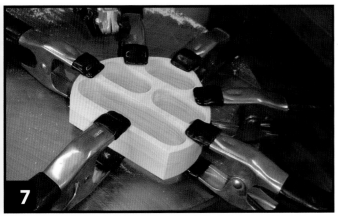

7

Place the two glued surfaces together and align all drawer openings and former blade entry holes. Clamp the two pieces together.

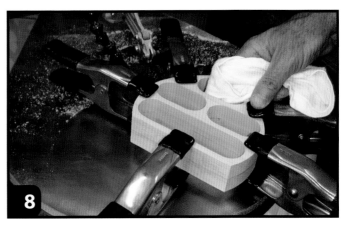

8

Use a rag to clean up glue squeeze-out. Leave the pieces clamped for one hour, and then unclamp them. Glue up remaining two box pieces, following Steps 4 to 8. Then, let the glue dry for both glue-ups.

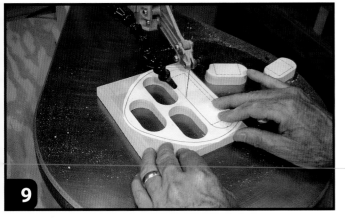

9

Adhere a pattern to the surfaced side of the ½" x 5¼" x 6" stock. Drill ¹⁄₁₆" blade entry holes, and use a #5 reverse-tooth blade to cut out the drawers.

10

At this point, you have cut five pieces for each drawer—four ¾"-thick pieces and one ½"-thick piece. All drawers are made from three ¾"-thick pieces and one ½"-thick drawer piece to allow for the solid ¼"-thick box back, so we will disgard one of the ¾"-thick pieces that we cut.

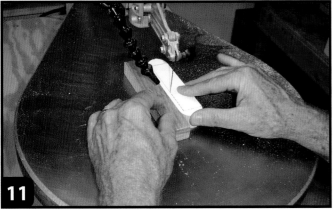

11

For each drawer, use a #9 reverse-tooth blade to cut out three ¾"-thick drawer compartments by cutting along the dashed lines. Then, use a #5 reverse-tooth blade to cut out one ½"-thick drawer compartment by cutting along dashed lines. Use a scrap of wood to support the pieces during cutting.

12

Remove patterns from all drawer pieces, and use a folded sheet of sandpaper to sand off the wood fuzzies.

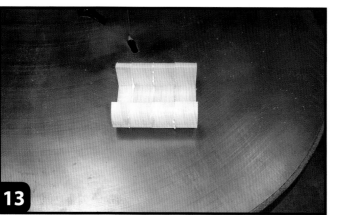

13

For each drawer, apply a thin layer of glue to three ¾"-thick drawer pieces and one ½"-thick drawer piece. Line up all four former blade entry holes on the same side of each drawer.

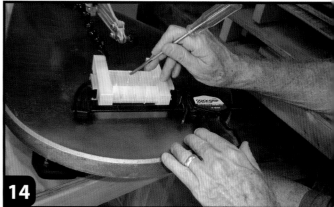

14

Using scrap wood blocks, clamp up all drawers. Use a flathead screwdriver to remove glue squeeze-out, and then let the glue dry.

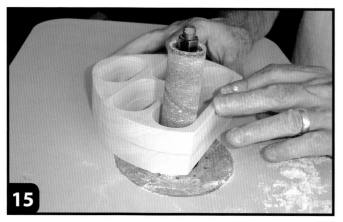

15

Use a drum sander or sandpaper wrapped around a wooden dowel to sand both box pieces smooth.

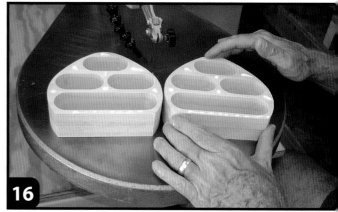

16

Put a thin layer of glue on both box pieces. Next, adhere the two pieces together by lining up the drawer openings. Wait about five minutes for the glue to set up before clamping.

17

Clamp up the two box pieces and let the glue dry.

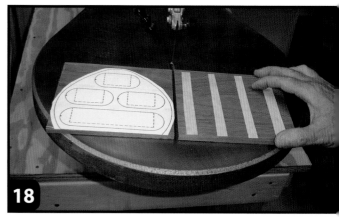

18

Adhere a box pattern to the surfaced edge of a ¼" x 5¼" x 6" piece of wood. Next, place several strips of double-sided tape on the second ¼" piece of wood. Then, adhere the two pieces together.

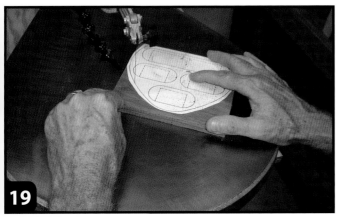

19

Use a #5 reverse-tooth blade to cut the outside profile of the box pattern. Then, detach the bottom piece of wood, which is the back of the box. Leave the pattern attached to the top piece.

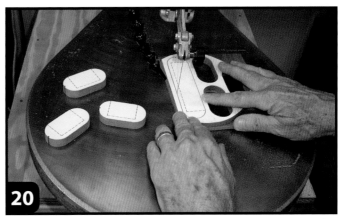

20

Attach the piece of wood with the pattern on top to the remaining ¼" x 5¼" x 6" piece of wood. Reuse the same double-sided tape. Then, drill ¹⁄₁₆" blade entry holes, and use a #5 reverse-tooth blade to cut out the drawer openings. Detach the two pieces of wood. These pieces are the front of the box and the fronts and backs of the drawers. Remove the patterns.

21

Sand the wood fuzzies off all of the ¼" pieces. Use a drum sander, as you did in Step 15, to sand the drawer openings smooth. Use a wooden block and sandpaper to sand the inside openings of all drawers. **Note:** If you are lining your drawers with felt or velvet, there is no need to sand the drawer bottoms—just sand the sides.

22

Glue the front and back to the box, and use masking tape to temporarily hold the front and back to the glued surfaces. Next, glue the fronts and backs to the drawers by keeping the former blade entry holes on the same side of the drawers. Then, use a screwdriver to remove glue squeeze-out.

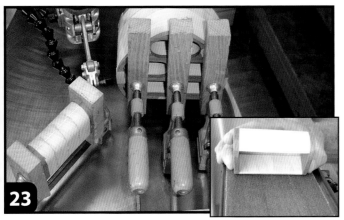

23

Clamp the box and drawers and allow the glue to dry. Then, sand the outside profile of the drawers and box.

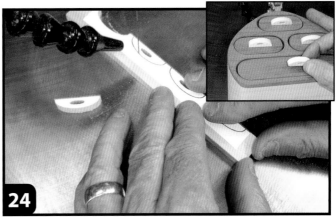

24

Adhere the drawer pull pattern that you like to the ¼" stock. Cut out any inside cuts, and then cut the outside profile of the pulls. Glue the drawer pulls onto the center of the drawers. Apply the finish of your choice, and line the drawer compartments with felt or velvet, as described in Chapter One, "Box-Making Basics," on page 5.

ROUND FOUR-DRAWER BOX

The round shape is easy to cut on your scroll saw, and, with contrasting drawer pulls, this box makes a unique gift item. The box is made from poplar, which is easy to cut; oak, which is harder to cut, is the box front and back. I used walnut for the drawer pulls.

Overall size: 5¾" long x 5½" high x 3½" deep
Wood: Oak, poplar, and walnut

TOOLS AND MATERIALS

- ◆ Six photocopies of the box pattern
- ◆ Temporary bond spray adhesive
- ◆ #9 reverse-tooth blade for cutting ¾"-thick stock and box profile
- ◆ #5 reverse-tooth blade for cutting ¼"- and ½"-thick stock
- ◆ Drill or drill press and ⅟₁₆" drill bit
- ◆ Clear packaging tape
- ◆ Mineral spirits
- ◆ Sandpaper, 80, 150, and 220 grit
- ◆ Drum sander or sandpaper wrapped around wooden dowel
- ◆ Wood glue
- ◆ Clamps and scrap wood blocks
- ◆ Rag, to wipe away excess glue
- ◆ Masking tape
- ◆ Screwdriver
- ◆ Double-sided tape
- ◆ Felt or velvet (optional, for lining)
- ◆ Finish of choice

STOCK

- ◆ Four pieces ¾" x 5¾" x 6¼" for box and drawers
- ◆ One piece ½" x 5¾" x 6¼" for drawers
- ◆ Three pieces ¼" x 5¾" x 6¼" for drawer fronts and and box front and back
- ◆ One piece ¼" x ¾" x 6" for drawer pulls

ROUND FOUR-DRAWER BOX

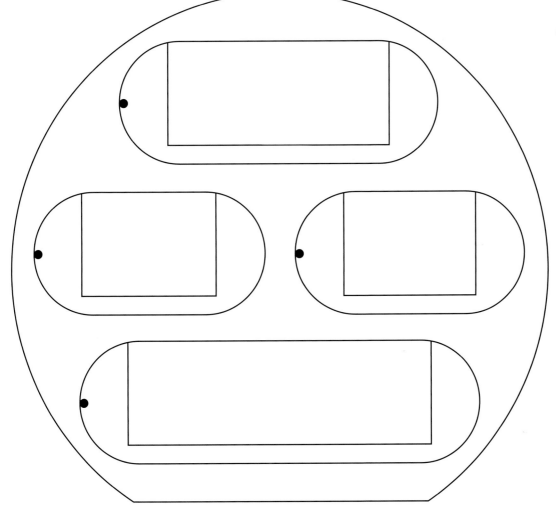

Box pattern

Make six photocopies of the box pattern.

Pattern dots indicate blade entry holes.

QUICK CUTS

BOX

◆ Cut out drawers and outside profile from four ¾" pieces of wood.

◆ Glue four box pieces together.

◆ Cut out drawers on ½" piece of wood.

◆ For each drawer, cut out three ¾" drawer compartments and one ½" drawer compartment, following dashed pattern lines.

◆ Glue each drawer together using three ¾"pieces and one ½" piece of wood.

◆ Using three ¼" pieces of wood, cut out box front and back and all of drawer fronts and backs.

◆ Select drawer pull pattern and cut out required number of drawer pulls.

◆ Glue drawer pulls to drawer fronts.

DRAWER PULLS

◆ Apply pattern to stock for number of drawer pulls needed.

◆ Tilt scroll saw table 10 degrees, right side down.

◆ Cut out drawer pulls, following cut direction arrows.

TALL BOX

This box has three drawers, but they are larger than the drawers for some of the other boxes. This box is easy to scroll, being made entirely of poplar with walnut drawer pulls.

Overall size: 3½" long x 5¾" high x 3½" deep
Wood: Poplar and walnut

TOOLS AND MATERIALS

- Six photocopies of the box pattern
- Temporary bond spray adhesive
- #9 reverse-tooth blade for cutting ¾"-thick stock and box profile
- #5 reverse-tooth blade for cutting ¼"- and ½"-thick stock
- Drill or drill press and 1⁄16" drill bit
- Clear packaging tape
- Mineral spirits
- Sandpaper, 80, 150, and 220 grit
- Drum sander or sandpaper wrapped around wooden dowel
- Wood glue
- Clamps and scrap wood blocks
- Rag, to wipe away excess glue
- Masking tape
- Screwdriver
- Double-sided tape
- Felt or velvet (optional, for lining)
- Finish of choice

STOCK

- Four pieces ¾" x 3¾" x 6¼" for box and drawers
- One piece ½" x 3¾" x 6¼" for drawers
- Three pieces ¼" x 3¾" x 6¼" for drawer fronts and b and box front and back
- One piece ¼" x ¾" x 4" for drawer pulls

TALL BOX

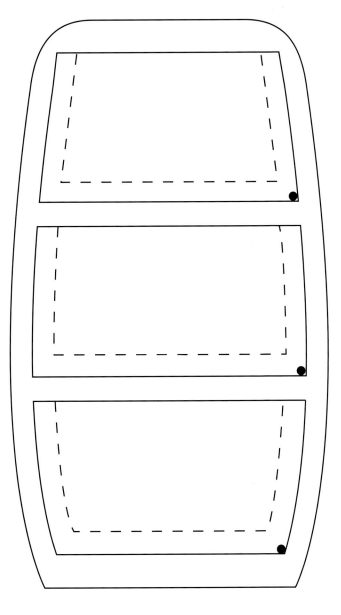

Box pattern

Make six photocopies
of the box pattern.

Pattern dots indicate
blade entry holes.

QUICK CUTS

BOX

- Cut out drawers and outside profile from four ¾" pieces of wood.
- Glue four box pieces together.
- Cut out drawers on ½" piece of wood.
- For each drawer, cut out three ¾" drawer compartments and one ½" drawer compartment, following dashed pattern lines.
- Glue each drawer together using three ¾" pieces and one ½" piece of wood.
- Using three ¼" pieces of wood, cut out box front and back and all of drawer fronts and backs.

- Select drawer pull pattern and cut out required number of drawer pulls.
- Glue drawer pulls to drawer fronts.

DRAWER PULLS

- Apply pattern to stock for number of drawer pulls needed.
- Tilt scroll saw table 10 degrees, right side down.
- Cut out drawer pulls, following cut direction arrows.

CURVES BOX

This is a small box with a uniquely curved outside shape and two drawers that follow the same curves as the outside profile of the box. The box is made from sassafras, a wood with a unique smell and a beautiful grain pattern, with a contrasting poplar front and back. The drawer pulls are made from walnut.

Overall size: 3½" long x 3¾" high x 3¾" deep
Wood: Poplar, sassafras, and walnut

TOOLS AND MATERIALS

- ◆ Six photocopies of the box pattern
- ◆ Temporary bond spray adhesive
- ◆ #9 reverse-tooth blade for cutting ¾"-thick stock and box profile
- ◆ #5 reverse-tooth blade for cutting ¼"- and ½"-thick stock
- ◆ Drill or drill press and ¹⁄₁₆" drill bit
- ◆ Clear packaging tape
- ◆ Mineral spirits
- ◆ Sandpaper, 80, 150, and 220 grit
- ◆ Drum sander or sandpaper wrapped around wooden dowel
- ◆ Wood glue
- ◆ Clamps and scrap wood blocks
- ◆ Rag, to wipe away excess glue
- ◆ Masking tape
- ◆ Screwdriver
- ◆ Double-sided tape
- ◆ Felt or velvet (optional, for lining)
- ◆ Finish of choice

STOCK

- ◆ Four pieces ¾" x 4" x 3¾" for box and drawers
- ◆ One piece ½" x 4" x 3¾" for drawers
- ◆ Three pieces ¼" x 4" x 3¾" for drawer fronts and ba and box front and back
- ◆ One piece ¼" x ¾" x 3" for drawer pulls

CURVES BOX

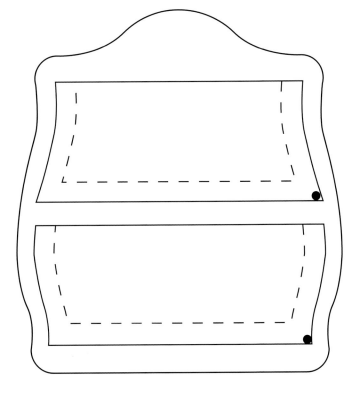

QUICK CUTS

BOX

- Cut out drawers and outside profile from four ¾" pieces of wood.
- Glue four box pieces together.
- Cut out drawers on ½" piece of wood.
- For each drawer, cut out three ¾" drawer compartments and one ½" drawer compartment, following dashed pattern lines.
- Glue each drawer together using three ¾" pieces and one ½" piece of wood.
- Using three ¼" pieces of wood, cut out box front and back and all of drawer fronts and backs.

- Select drawer pull pattern and cut out required number of drawer pulls.
- Glue drawer pulls to drawer fronts.

DRAWER PULLS

- Apply pattern to stock for number of drawer pulls needed.
- Tilt scroll saw table 10 degrees, right side down.
- Cut out drawer pulls, following cut direction arrows.

ROUND THREE-DRAWER BOX

This round-shaped box makes a great box for storing small items and has contrasting wood for the drawer pulls. The box is made from alder, the box front and back are made from poplar, and the drawer pulls are made from walnut.

Overall size: 5¼" long x 4⅜" high x 3½" deep
Wood: Alder, poplar, and walnut

TOOLS AND MATERIALS

- ◆ Six photocopies of the box pattern
- ◆ Temporary bond spray adhesive
- ◆ #9 reverse-tooth blade for cutting ¾"-thick stock and box profile
- ◆ #5 reverse-tooth blade for cutting ¼"- and ½"-thick stock
- ◆ Drill or drill press and ¹⁄₁₆" drill bit
- ◆ Clear packaging tape
- ◆ Mineral spirits
- ◆ Sandpaper, 80, 150, and 220 grit
- ◆ Drum sander or sandpaper wrapped around wooden dowel
- ◆ Wood glue
- ◆ Clamps and scrap wood blocks
- ◆ Rag, to wipe away excess glue
- ◆ Masking tape
- ◆ Screwdriver
- ◆ Double-sided tape
- ◆ Felt or velvet (optional, for lining)
- ◆ Finish of choice

STOCK

- ◆ Four pieces ¾" x 4½" x 5½" for box and drawers
- ◆ One piece ½" x 4½" x 5½" for drawers
- ◆ Three pieces ¼" x 4½" x 5½" for drawer fronts and ▶ and box front and back
- ◆ One piece ¼" x ¾" x 4" for drawer pulls

ROUND THREE-DRAWER BOX

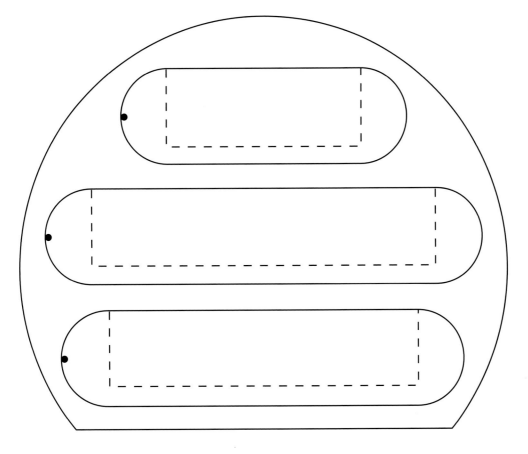

QUICK CUTS

BOX

- Cut out drawers and outside profile from four ¾" pieces of wood.

- Glue four box pieces together.

- Cut out drawers on ½" piece
of wood.

- For each drawer, cut out three
¾" drawer compartments and
one ½" drawer compartment,
following dashed pattern lines.

- Glue each drawer together using
three ¾" pieces and one ½" piece
of wood.

- Using three ¼" pieces of wood, cut
out box front and back and all of
drawer fronts and backs.

- Select drawer pull pattern and
cut out required number of
drawer pulls.

- Glue drawer pulls to drawer fronts.

DRAWER PULLS

- Apply pattern to stock for number
of drawer pulls needed.

- Tilt scroll saw table 10 degrees,
right side down.

- Cut out drawer pulls, following cut
direction arrows.

FLAT-TOP BOX

The shape of this box is more traditional for jewelry boxes. I used two woods—oak and maple—to make this box, which are harder to cut on a scroll saw than most woods. Walnut was used for the drawer pulls.

Overall size: 5¾" long x 3¼" high x 3½" deep

Wood: Maple, oak, and walnut

TOOLS AND MATERIALS

- Six photocopies of the box pattern
- Temporary bond spray adhesive
- #9 reverse-tooth blade for cutting ¾"-thick stock and box profile
- #5 reverse-tooth blade for cutting ¼"- and ½"-thick stock
- Drill or drill press and ⅟₁₆" drill bit
- Clear packaging tape
- Mineral spirits
- Sandpaper, 80, 150, and 220 grit
- Drum sander or sandpaper wrapped around wooden dowel
- Wood glue
- Clamps and scrap wood blocks
- Rag, to wipe away excess glue
- Masking tape
- Screwdriver
- Double-sided tape
- Felt or velvet (optional, for lining)
- Finish of choice

STOCK

- Four pieces ¾" x 3½" x 6" for box and drawers
- One piece ½" x 3½" x 6" for drawers
- Three pieces ¼" x 3½" x 6" for drawer fronts and b[a] and box front and back
- One piece ¼" x ¾" x 4" for drawer pulls

Box pattern

Make six photocopies
of the box pattern.

Pattern dots indicate
blade entry holes.

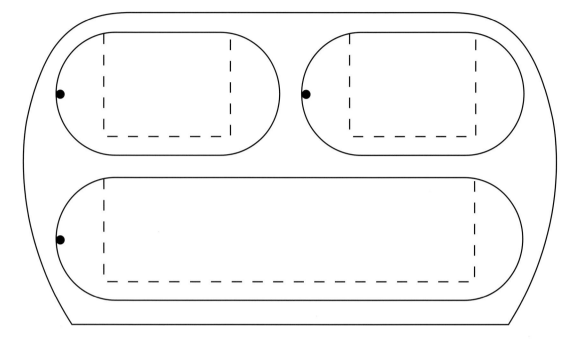

QUICK CUTS

BOX

◆ Cut out drawers and outside
profile from four ¾" pieces
of wood.

◆ Glue four box pieces together.

◆ Cut out drawers on ½" piece
of wood.

◆ For each drawer, cut out three
¾" drawer compartments and
one ½" drawer compartment,
following dashed pattern lines.

◆ Glue each drawer together using
three ¾" pieces and one
½" piece of wood.

◆ Using three ¼" pieces of wood,
cut out box front and back and
all of drawer fronts and backs.

◆ Select drawer pull pattern and
cut out required number of
drawer pulls.

◆ Glue drawer pulls to drawer
fronts.

DRAWER PULLS

◆ Apply pattern to stock for
number of drawer pulls needed.

◆ Tilt scroll saw table 10 degrees,
right side down.

◆ Cut out drawer pulls, following
cut direction arrows.

MAKING LAMINATED BOXES

These boxes are the result of my creating a quilt square design in a box lid a few years ago. My experiments with laminated wood of alternating light and dark colors stacked on top of each other produced a checkerboard design. Other designs followed: diamond, pie piece, and pinwheel shapes. When you stack cut layers of wood on the scroll saw, you get a very tight glue joint on the adjacent pieces of wood that are cut. By gluing together several checkerboard or other designs, you can build box blanks. You can cut out a compartment on the box blank, glue on a box bottom layer, and you have built your box. Many design shapes are possible in addition to the ones that appear in this book.

Precision pinpoint pattern placement, explained on page 4, is a great way to accurately apply patterns right in the center of the stock. This technique is especially helpful when you are working with laminated stock because it helps space the contrasting woods equally within the pattern. I usually don't line the compartments on these boxes since the designs on the insides of the boxes are symmetrical.

All of the boxes in this chapter are made by using ½"-thick wood, stack cutting the wood, and gluing up the pieces in the appropriate design. Each box is made from six laminated layers. The following pages take you through the steps of making laminated boxes.

CHECKERBOARD OVAL BOX

This box has fancy-shaped compartments, and the checkerboard pattern is perfect from the box to the lid. I used poplar and walnut to make the checkerboard laminations.

Overall size: 5½" long x
2½" high x 4" deep
Wood: Poplar and walnut

LAMINATION QUICK CUTS

◆ Three photocopies of the checkerboard lamination pattern on page 59

◆ Gluing jig (see page 3)

◆ Newspaper, to protect gluing jig surface

◆ Six clamping blocks

◆ Rag, to wipe away excess glue

◆ One photocopy each of the box, lid, and lid liner patterns

◆ Temporary bond spray adhesive

◆ Pencil

◆ #5 reverse-tooth blade for cutting ½"-thick wood

◆ Thick-wood or #12 reverse-tooth blade for cutting thick wood

◆ Drill or drill press and ⅛" drill bit

◆ Double-sided tape

◆ Clear packaging tape

◆ Sandpaper, 80, 150, and 220 grit

◆ Belt sander (optional)

◆ Wood glue

◆ Three screw clamps

◆ Masking tape

◆ Felt or velvet (optional, for lining)

◆ Finish of choice

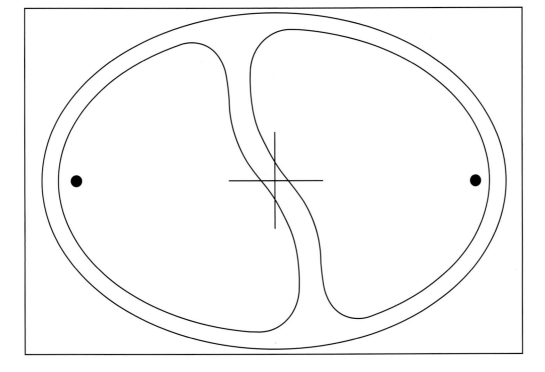

Box pattern

Make one photocopy
of the box pattern.

Pattern dots indicate
blade entry holes.

Enlarge pattern 110%

Lid pattern

Make one photocopy
of the lid pattern.

Enlarge pattern 110%

STOCK

- Six pieces ½" x 1" x 13" light-colored wood for box laminations

- Six pieces ½" x 1" x 13" dark-colored wood for box laminations

- Four pieces ½" x 4" x 6½" laminated wood for box and box bottom

- One piece ½" x 4" x 6½" laminated wood for lid

- One piece ½" x 4" x 6½" laminated wood for lid liners

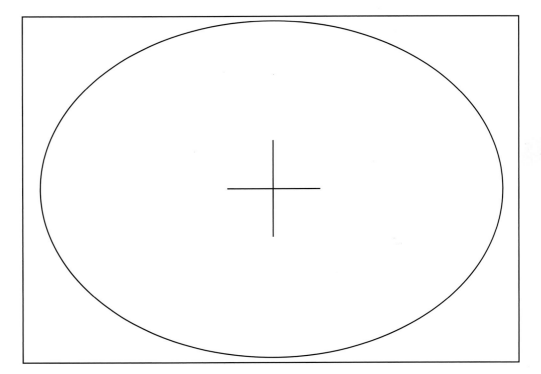

Lid liner pattern
Make one photocopy of the
lid liner pattern.

Enlarge pattern 110%

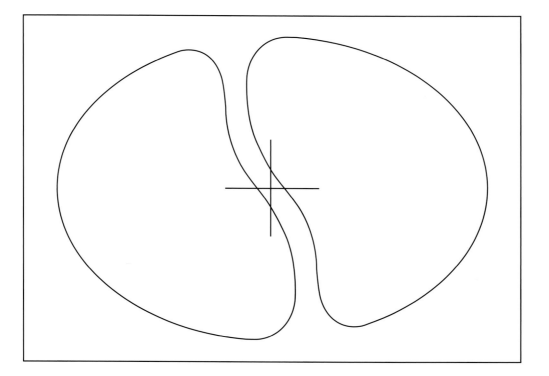

QUICK CUTS

BOX

◆ Glue three ½" x 4" x 6½"
laminated layers together,
arranging layers in checkerboard
design on sides.

◆ Adhere box pattern to stock,
using pin to center pattern.

◆ Drill two holes as indicated
on pattern.

◆ Cut out both compartments.

◆ For box bottom, glue one
½" x 4" x 6½" laminated layer
to the box, arranging layer in
checkerboard design.

LID

◆ Apply pattern to stock.

◆ Cut around the pattern line
for lid.

LID LINERS

◆ Use pin to center pattern
on stock.

◆ Cut lid liners on pattern lines.

◆ Place lid liners into box
compartments.

◆ Place lid on top of box, arranged
in checkerboard design.

◆ Turn box over and remove box
from lid.

◆ Glue liners in place.

◆ Clamp with spring-type clamps.

CHECKERBOARD OVAL BOX

1	2	3	4	5	6

LAMINATION QUICK CUTS

- Glue up four pieces of wood on the gluing jig, alternating light and dark woods.
- Leave the wood glued together for one hour; then, glue up two more laminations.
- Cut the three laminated pieces of wood in half to yield six 6½" pieces of wood
- Use double-sided tape to adhere two ½" x 4" x 6½" laminated pieces of wood together.
- Alternate the two pieces of wood so that dark and light wood laminations are adhered together.

- Adhere the pattern and make five cuts along pattern lines.
- Separate the pieces numbered 1 through 6, alternating pieces to make checkerboard laminations.
- Glue six pieces of wood in a checkerboard design on the gluing jig.
- Cut and glue up the remaining wood for the six checkerboard laminations.
- Use a belt sander to sand the six laminations flat and smooth.

1

Glue up four pieces of ½" x 1" x 13" wood on the gluing jig, alternating light and dark woods. Protect the gluing jig surface with newspaper. Use clamping blocks and leave the wood clamped in the jig for one hour. Then, use a rag to wipe up glue squeeze-out. Do two more glue-ups, and let the glue dry on all three pieces.

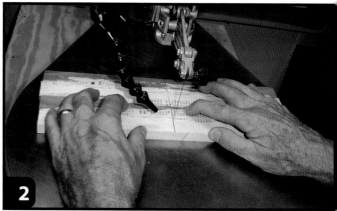

2

Take the newspaper off your three laminated pieces of wood. Use a #5 reverse-tooth blade to cut the three pieces of wood in half to yield six 6½" pieces of wood. Then, use 80-grit sandpaper to sand off the dried glue and newspaper from the six 6½" pieces of wood.

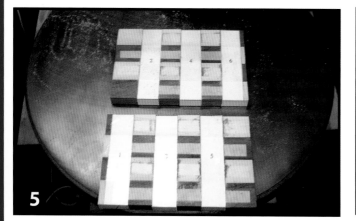

3

Use double-sided tape to adhere two ½" x 4" x 6½" laminated pieces of wood stacked together. Alternate the two pieces of wood so that light and dark wood laminations are adhered together. You'll have three stacks, each with two layers.

4

Adhere a checkerboard lamination pattern to the stacked pieces of wood. Cover the pattern with clear packaging tape. Then, use a #12 reverse-tooth blade to make five cuts along pattern lines on each of the three stacks.

5

Separate the pieces numbered 1 through 6, alternating pieces to make checkerboard laminations. Keep all six pieces in numerical order (from 1 to 6). Next, use a pencil to mark the pieces in numerical order.

6

Remove the tape and patterns. Use a piece of folded sandpaper to sand off the wood fuzzies. Remove any sawdust.

7

Use the gluing jig to glue up six pieces of wood to make a checkerboard design. Protect the jig surface with newspaper, and clean up glue squeeze-out with a rag. Leave the wood clamped for one hour. Then, glue up the remaining five laminations, and let the glue dry.

8

Use a belt sander to sand the six laminations smooth and flat. If you don't have a belt sander, you can hand sand the pieces with 80-grit sandpaper.

9

Glue up three layers, arranging the edge pattern in a checkerboard design. Clamp the three layers together, and let the glue dry.

10

Spray the back of the box pattern with spray adhesive. Use the precision pinpoint pattern placement technique to center the pattern on the stock (see page 4 for more information). Cover the pattern with clear packaging tape.

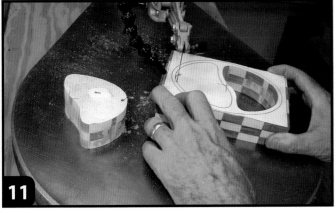

11

Drill two 1/8" blade entry holes where indicated on pattern. Cut out the two compartments, following pattern lines.

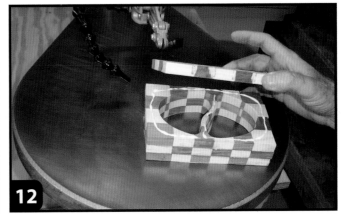

12

Use a piece of folded sandpaper to sand the wood fuzzies from the bottom of the box. Apply glue to the box bottom. Then, place a layer of laminated wood on the glued surface, arranging the layer in a checkerboard design.

13 Use masking tape to temporarily hold the box bottom in place on the box.

14 Clamp the box bottom onto the box. Let the glue dry.

15 Adhere the lid pattern to a laminated wood layer. Next, center the pattern on the stock with a pin as you did in Step 10, and cover the pattern with clear tape. Then, use a #5 reverse-tooth blade to cut out the lid, following the pattern line.

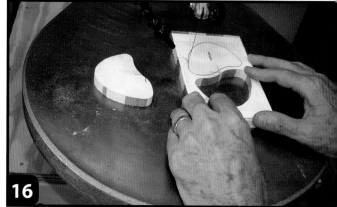

16 Adhere the lid liner pattern to another laminated wood layer. Next, center the lid liner pattern as you did the previous step, and cover the pattern with clear tape. Then, use a #5 reverse-tooth blade to cut out two lid liners, following pattern lines.

17 Cut the outside profile of the box, following the pattern line. Remove the box pattern.

18 Remove the lid liner patterns. Place the lid liners into the box compartments.

Remove the lid pattern. Place the lid onto the top of the box matching the checkerboard design.

Turn the box upside down, and remove the box from the lid. Glue the lid liners in this position, testing the box for fit over the lid liners.

Use spring-type clamps to clamp the lid liners onto the lid, and let the glue dry. Sand the box and lid smooth; then, apply a finish of your choice.

CHECKERBOARD HORSESHOE BOX

This box has horseshoe-shaped compartments that are very symmetrical when cut on a scroll saw. Pattern placement using a pin is important to make both horseshoe compartments symmetrical using poplar and walnut.

Overall size: 6" long x 2½" high x 4" deep
Wood: Poplar and walnut

TOOLS AND MATERIALS

- Three photocopies of the checkerboard lamination pattern on page 59
- Gluing jig (see page 3)
- Newspaper, to protect gluing jig surface
- Six clamping blocks
- Rag, to wipe away excess glue
- One photocopy each of the box, lid, and lid liner patterns
- Temporary bond spray adhesive
- Pencil
- #5 reverse-tooth blade for cutting ½"-thick wood
- Thick-wood or #12 reverse-tooth blade for cutting thick wood
- Drill or drill press and ⅛" drill bit
- Double-sided tape
- Clear packaging tape
- Sandpaper, 80, 150, and 220 grit
- Belt sander (optional)
- Wood glue
- Three screw clamps
- Masking tape
- Felt or velvet (optional, for lining)
- Finish of choice

CHECKERBOARD HORSESHOE BOX

STOCK

◆ Six pieces ½" x 1" x 13" light-colored wood for box laminations

◆ Six pieces ½" x 1" x 13" dark-colored wood for box laminations

◆ Four pieces ½" x 4" x 6½" laminated wood for box and box bottom

◆ One piece ½" x 4" x 6½" laminated wood for lid

◆ One piece ½" x 4" x 6½" laminated wood for lid liners

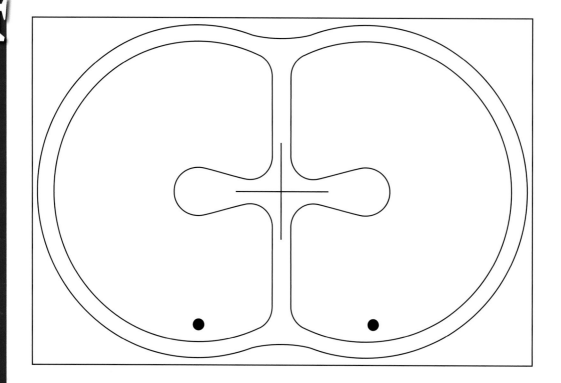

Box pattern

Make one photocopy of the box pattern.

Pattern dots indicate blade entry holes.

Enlarge pattern 110%

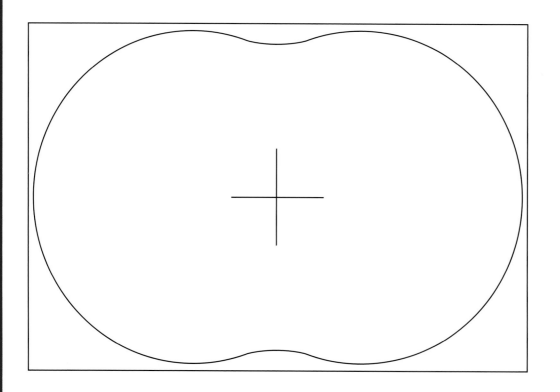

Lid pattern

Make one photocopy of the lid pattern.

Enlarge pattern 110%

CHECKERBOARD HORSESHOE BOX

Lid liner pattern

Make one photocopy
of the lid liner pattern.

Enlarge pattern 110%

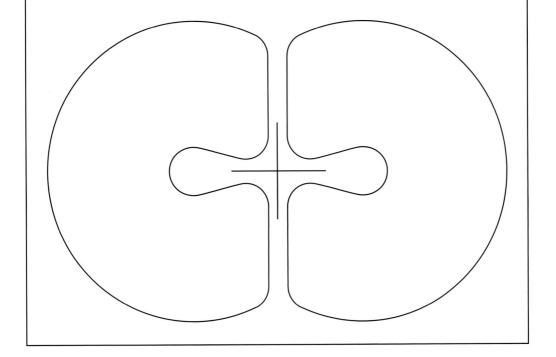

QUICK CUTS

BOX

- ◆ Glue three ½" x 4" x 6½" laminated layers together, arranging layers in checkerboard design on sides.
- ◆ Adhere box pattern to stock, using pin to center pattern.
- ◆ Drill two ⅛" holes as indicated on pattern.
- ◆ Cut out both compartments.
- ◆ For box bottom, glue one ½" x 4" x 6½" laminated layer onto box, arranging layer in checkerboard design.

LID

- ◆ Use pin to center pattern on stock.
- ◆ Cut lid on pattern line.

LID LINERS

- ◆ Use pin to center pattern on stock.
- ◆ Cut lid liners on pattern lines.
- ◆ Place lid liners into box compartments.
- ◆ Place lid on top of box, arranged in checkerboard design.
- ◆ Turn box over and remove box from lid.
- ◆ Glue lid liners in place.
- ◆ Clamp with spring-type clamps.

DIAMOND BOX

This box shows that you can make a box from shapes other than a checkerboard. Made from poplar and walnut, the diamond-shaped laminations are easy to cut on a scroll saw.

TOOLS AND MATERIALS

- ◆ Three photocopies of the diamond lamination pattern on page 71
- ◆ Gluing jig (see page 3)
- ◆ Newspaper, to protect gluing jig surface
- ◆ Six clamping blocks
- ◆ Rag, to wipe away excess glue
- ◆ One photocopy each of the box, lid, and lid liner patterns
- ◆ Temporary bond spray adhesive
- ◆ Pencil
- ◆ #5 reverse-tooth blade for cutting ½"-thick wood
- ◆ Thick-wood or #12 reverse-tooth blade for cutting thick wood
- ◆ Drill or drill press and ⅛" drill bit
- ◆ Double-sided tape
- ◆ Clear packaging tape
- ◆ Sandpaper, 80, 150, and 220 grit
- ◆ Belt sander (optional)
- ◆ Wood glue
- ◆ Three screw clamps
- ◆ Masking tape
- ◆ Felt or velvet (optional, for lining)
- ◆ Finish of choice

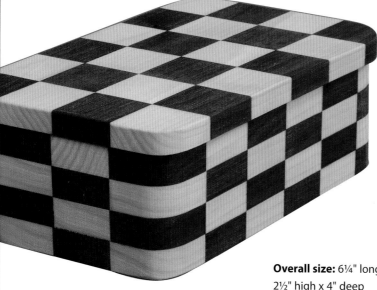

Overall size: 6¼" long x 2½" high x 4" deep
Wood: Poplar and walnut

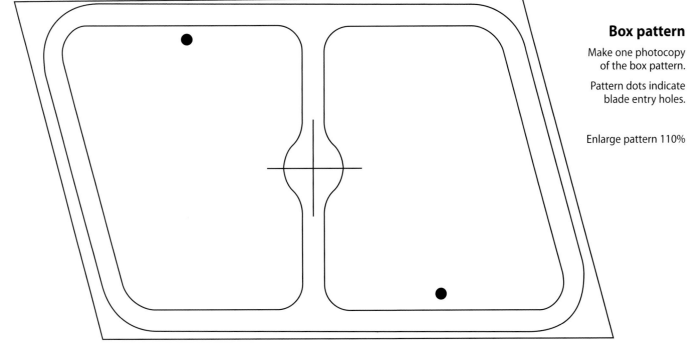

Box pattern

Make one photocopy
of the box pattern.

Pattern dots indicate
blade entry holes.

Enlarge pattern 110%

STOCK

- Six pieces ½" x 1" x 15" light-colored wood for box laminations
- Six pieces ½" x 1" x 15" dark-colored wood for box laminations
- Four pieces ½" x 4" x 7½" laminated wood for box and box bottom
- One piece ½" x 4" x 7½" laminated wood for lid
- One piece ½" x 4" x 7½" laminated wood for lid liners

Lid pattern

Make one photocopy
of the lid pattern.

Enlarge pattern 110%

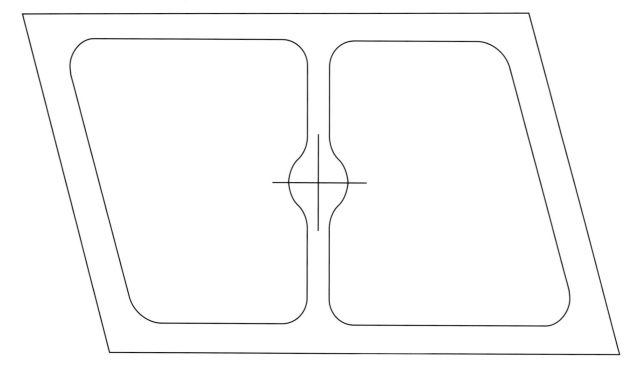

QUICK CUTS

BOX

◆ Glue three ½" x 4" x 7½"
laminated layers together,
arranging layers in diamond
design on sides.

◆ Adhere box pattern to stock,
using pin to center pattern.

◆ Drill two ⅛" holes as indicated
on pattern.

◆ Cut out both compartments.

◆ For box bottom, glue one
½" x 4" x 7½" laminated layer
to box, arranging layer in
diamond design.

LID

◆ Use pin to center pattern
on stock.

◆ Cut lid on pattern line.

LID LINERS

◆ Use pin to center pattern on
stock.

◆ Cut lid liners on pattern lines.

◆ Place lid liners into
box compartments.

◆ Place lid on top of box, arranged
in diamond design.

◆ Turn box over and remove box
from lid.

◆ Glue lid liners in place.

◆ Clamp with spring-type clamps.

DIAMOND BOX

Diamond lamination pattern

Make three photocopies of the
lamination pattern.

Enlarge pattern 110%

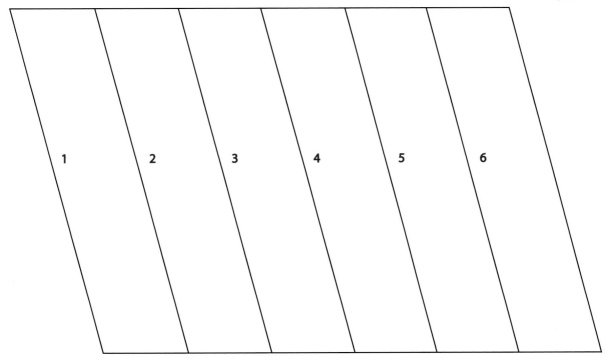

LAMINATION QUICK CUTS

◆ Glue up four pieces of wood on the gluing jig, alternating light and dark woods.

◆ Leave the wood glued together for one hour; Then, glue up two more laminations.

◆ Cut the three laminated pieces of wood in half to yield six 7½" pieces of wood.

◆ Use double-sided tape to adhere two ½" x 4" x 7½" laminated pieces of wood together.

◆ Alternate the two pieces of wood so that dark and light wood laminations are adhered together.

◆ Adhere the pattern and make five cuts along pattern lines.

◆ Separate the pieces numbered 1 through 6, alternating pieces to make two diamond laminations.

◆ Glue six pieces of wood in a diamond design on the gluing jig.

◆ Cut and glue up the remaining wood for the six diamond laminations.

◆ Use a belt sander to sand the six laminations flat and smooth.

FOUR WOODS BOX

This box shows that you can make a box with laminations of any size. I used four different woods—ash, cherry, oak, and poplar—for a contrasting woods box.

Overall size: 7¾" long x 2½" high x 4" deep
Wood: Ash, cherry, oak, and poplar

TOOLS AND MATERIALS

- Three photocopies of the four woods lamination pattern on page 75
- Gluing jig (see page 3)
- Newspaper, to protect gluing jig surface
- Six clamping blocks
- Rag, to wipe away excess glue
- One photocopy each of the box, lid, and lid liner patterns
- Temporary bond spray adhesive
- Pencil
- #5 reverse-tooth blade for cutting ½"-thick wood
- Thick-wood or #12 reverse-tooth blade for cutting wood
- Drill or drill press and ⅛" drill bit
- Double-sided tape
- Clear packaging tape
- Sandpaper, 80, 150, and 220 grit
- Belt sander (optional)
- Wood glue
- Three screw clamps
- Masking tape
- Felt or velvet (optional, for lining)
- Finish of choice

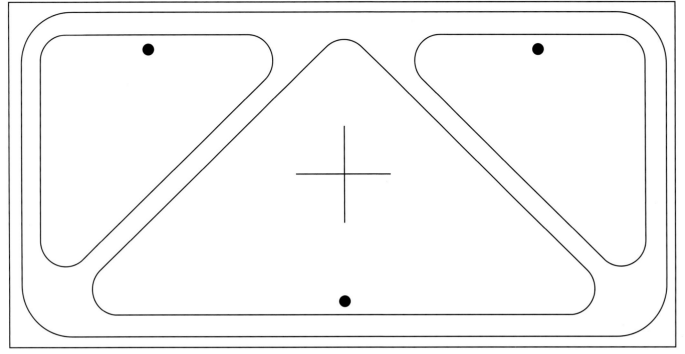

Box pattern   Make one photocopy of the box pattern. Pattern dots indicate blade entry holes. Enlarge pattern 110%

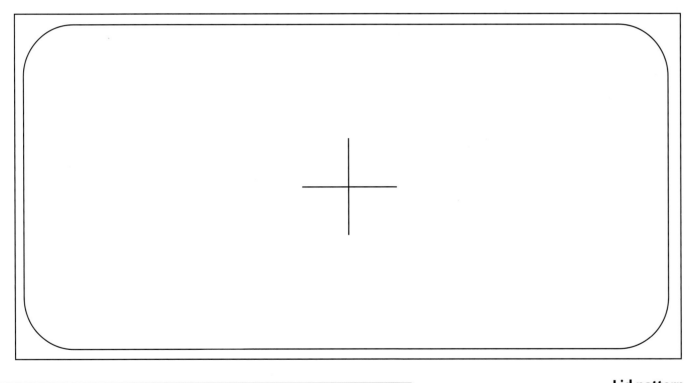

Lid pattern

Make one photocopy
of the lid pattern.

Enlarge pattern 110%

STOCK

◆ Three pieces ½" x 1" x 17" wood species #1
◆ Three pieces ½" x 1" x 17" wood species #2
◆ Three pieces ½" x 1" x 17" wood species #3
◆ Three pieces ½" x 1" x 17" wood species #4
◆ Four pieces ½" x 4" x 8½" laminated wood for box and box bottom
◆ One piece ½" x 4" x 8½" laminated wood for lid
◆ One piece ½" x 4" x 8½" laminated wood for lid liners

Lid liner pattern

Make one photocopy of the
lid liner pattern.

Enlarge pattern 110%

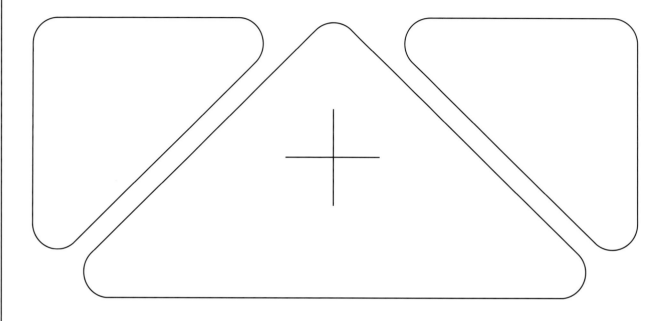

QUICK CUTS

BOX

◆ Glue three ½" x 4" x 8½"
laminated layers together,
arranging the layers in checkerboard design on the sides.

◆ Adhere box pattern to stock
using pin to center pattern.

◆ Drill three ⅛" holes as indicated
on pattern.

◆ Cut out compartments.

◆ For box bottom, glue one
½" x 4" x 8½" laminated layer
to box, arranging layer in
checkerboard design.

LID

◆ Use pin to center pattern
on stock.

◆ Cut lid on pattern line.

LID LINERS

◆ Use pin to center pattern
on stock.

◆ Cut lid liners on pattern lines.

◆ Place lid liners into
box compartments.

◆ Place lid on top of box, arranged
in checkerboard design.

◆ Turn box over and remove box
from lid.

◆ Glue lid liners in place.

◆ Clamp with spring-type clamps.

FOUR WOODS BOX

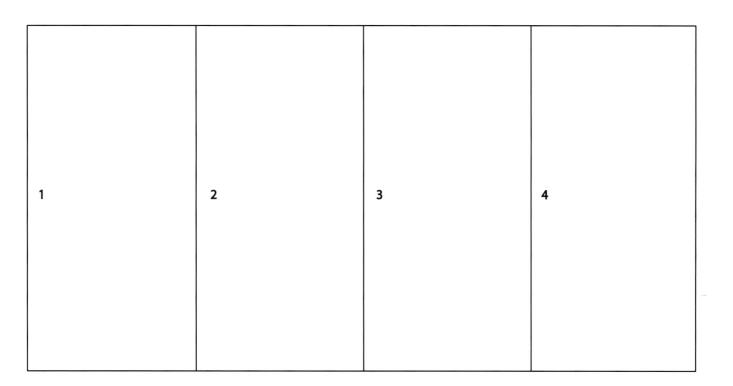

| 1 | 2 | 3 | 4 |

LAMINATION QUICK CUTS

◆ Glue up four pieces of wood on the gluing jig, wood species #1, #2, #3, and #4.

◆ Leave the wood glued together for one hour; then, glue up two more laminations in the same wood species order #1, #2, #3, and #4.

◆ Cut the three laminated pieces of wood in half to yield six 8½" pieces of wood.

◆ Use double-sided tape to adhere two ½" x 4" x 8½" laminated pieces of wood together.

◆ Alternate the two pieces of wood so that the same wood species are not adhered together.

◆ Adhere the pattern and make three cuts along pattern lines.

◆ Separate the pieces numbered 1 through 4, alternating pieces to make two checkerboard design laminations.

◆ Glue four pieces of wood in a checkerboard design on the gluing jig.

◆ Cut and glue up the remaining wood for the six checkerboard laminations.

◆ Use a belt sander to sand the six laminations flat and smooth.

PINWHEEL BOX

This round box has a pinwheel-shaped lid pattern and a checkerboard box profile on the sides. Pattern placement using a pin is important for this box made from poplar and walnut.

Overall size: 5" long x 2½" high x 5" deep
Wood: Poplar and walnut

TOOLS AND MATERIALS

- Eight photocopies of the pinwheel lamination pattern on page 79 (**Note:** Lamination pattern doubles as lid pattern.)
- Gluing jig (see page 3)
- Newspaper, to protect gluing jig surface
- Six clamping blocks
- Rag, to wipe away excess glue
- One photocopy each of the box, lid, and lid liner patterns
- Temporary bond spray adhesive
- Pencil
- #5 reverse-tooth blade for cutting ½"-thick wood
- Thick-wood or #12 reverse-tooth blade for cutting thick wood
- Drill or drill press and ⅛" drill bit
- Double-sided tape
- Clear packaging tape
- Sandpaper, 80, 150, and 220 grit
- Belt sander (optional)
- Wood glue
- Three screw clamps
- Masking tape
- Felt or velvet (optional, for lining)
- Finish of choice

OCK

Three pieces ½" x 5½" x 5½" ight-colored wood

Three pieces ½" x 5½" x 5½" dark-colored wood

Four pieces ½" x 5" x 5" aminated wood for box and box bottom

One piece ½" x 5" x 5" for lid

One piece ½" x 5½" x 5½" aminated wood for lid liners

Box pattern

Make one photocopy of the box pattern.

Pattern dots indicate blade entry holes.

Enlarge pattern 110%

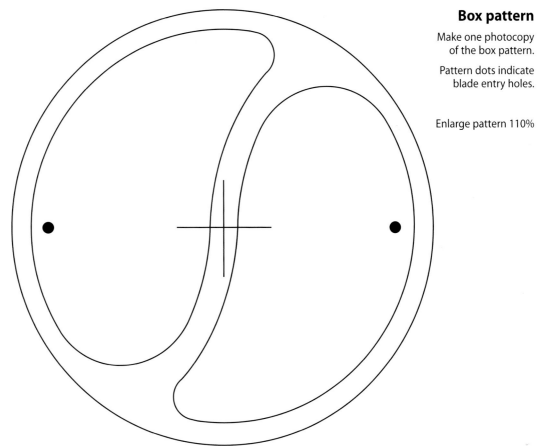

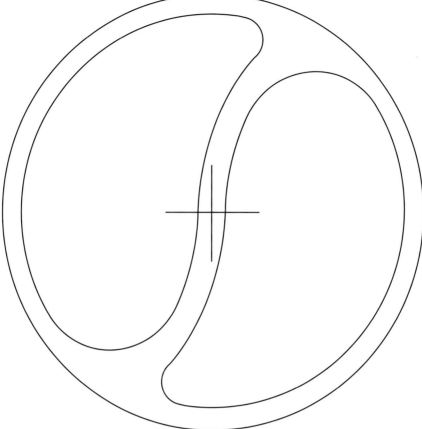

QUICK CUTS

BOX

◆ Glue three ½" x 5" x 5" laminated
layers together, arranging
pinwheel direction the same for
all layers and arranging layers in
checkerboard design.

◆ Adhere box pattern to stock,
using pin to center pattern.

◆ Drill two ⅛" holes as indicated
on pattern.

◆ Cut out compartments.

◆ For box bottom, glue one
½" x 5" x 5" laminated layer onto
the box, arranging pinwheel
direction the same as other layers
and arranging box bottom in
checkerboard design.

LID LINERS

◆ Use pin to center pattern on
½" x 5½" x 5½" stock, arranging
pinwheel direction the same as
other layers.

◆ Cut lid liners on pattern lines.

◆ Place lid liners into box
compartments.

◆ Place lid on top of box, arranging
pinwheel direction the same as
other layers and arranging lid in
checkerboard design.

◆ Turn box over and remove box
from lid.

◆ Glue lid liners in place.

◆ Clamp with spring-type clamps.

PINWHEEL BOX

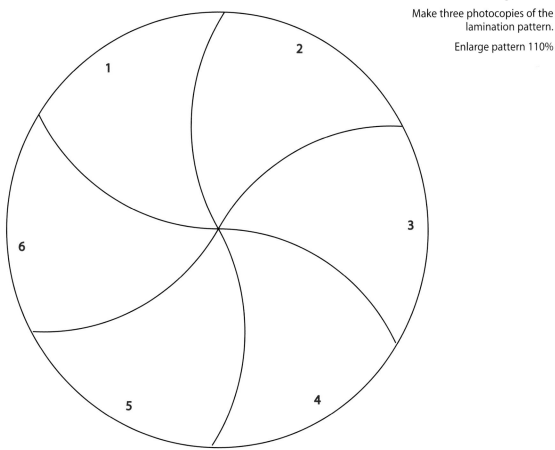

LAMINATION QUICK CUTS

- Use double-sided tape to adhere one light-colored piece and one dark-colored piece of wood together.

- Adhere the pattern and make a cut from the outside edge through the middle to the other edge of the pattern, following the pattern line.

- Make four cuts from the outside edge toward the middle of the pattern, following pattern lines.

- Separate the pieces numbered 1 through 6, alternating the pieces to make two pinwheel design laminations.

- Glue six pieces of wood in a pinwheel design on the gluing jig.

- Cut and glue up the remaining wood for the six pinwheel laminations.

- Use a belt sander to sand the six pinwheel laminations flat and smooth.

- Adhere a pattern to each of the five pinwheel laminations, using a pin to center patterns.

- Cut the outside edge of the patterns for the five pinwheel laminations.

PIE SEGMENT BOX

I made this round box from pie-piece-shaped laminations, and the box sides have a checkerboard profile. I used poplar and walnut to make this box.

Overall size: 5" long x
2½" high x 5" deep
Wood: Poplar and walnut

TOOLS AND MATERIALS

◆ Eight photocopies of the pie segment lamination pattern on page 83 (**Note:** Lamination pattern also doubles as lid pattern.)

◆ Gluing jig (see page 3)

◆ Newspaper, to protect gluing jig surface

◆ Six clamping blocks

◆ Rag, to wipe away excess glue

◆ One photocopy each of the box, lid, and lid liner patterns

◆ Temporary bond spray adhesive

◆ Pencil

◆ #5 reverse-tooth blade for cutting ½"-thick wood

◆ Thick-wood or #12 reverse-tooth blade for cutting thick wood

◆ Drill or drill press and ⅛" drill bit

◆ Double-sided tape

◆ Clear packaging tape

◆ Sandpaper, 80, 150, and 220 grit

◆ Belt sander (optional)

◆ Wood glue

◆ Three screw clamps

◆ Masking tape

◆ Felt or velvet (optional, for lining)

◆ Finish of choice

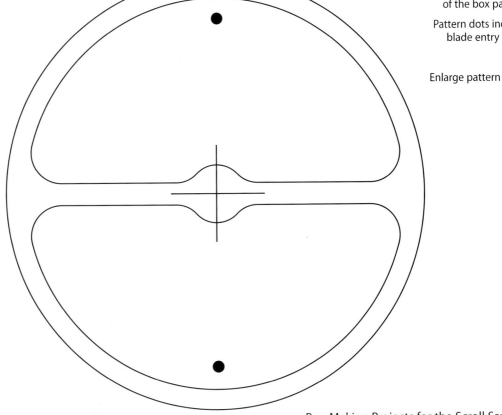

ГОСК

Three pieces ½" x 5½" x 5½"
light-colored wood

Three pieces ½" x 5½" x 5½"
dark-colored wood

Four pieces ½" x 5" x 5"
laminated wood for box and
box bottom

One piece ½" x 5" x 5" for lid

One piece ½" x 5½" x 5½"
laminated wood for lid liner

Box pattern

Make one photocopy
of the box pattern.

Pattern dots indicate
blade entry holes.

Enlarge pattern 110%

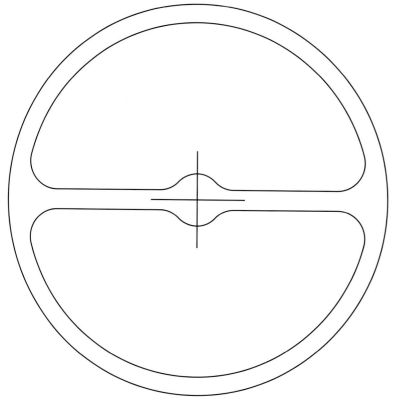

QUICK CUTS

BOX

◆ Glue three ½" x 5" x 5" laminated layers together, arranging layers in checkerboard design.

◆ Adhere box pattern to stock, using pin to center pattern.

◆ Drill two ⅛" holes as indicated on pattern.

◆ Cut out compartments.

◆ For box bottom, glue one ½" x 5" x 5" laminated layer to box, arranging box bottom in checkerboard design.

LID LINERS

◆ Use a pin to center pattern on ½" x 5½" x 5½" stock.

◆ Cut lid liners on pattern lines.

◆ Place lid liners into box compartments.

◆ Place lid on top of box, arranging lid i checkerboard design.

◆ Turn box over and remove box from lid.

◆ Glue lid liners in place.

◆ Clamp with spring-type clamps.

PIE SEGMENT BOX

Pie segment lamination pattern

Make three photocopies of the lamination pattern.

Enlarge pattern 110%

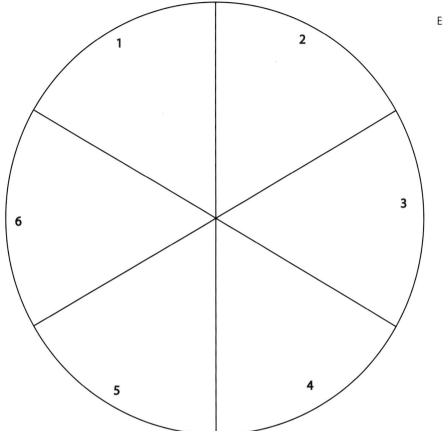

LAMINATION QUICK CUTS

- Use double-sided tape to adhere one light-colored piece and one dark-colored piece of wood together.

- Adhere the pattern and make a cut from the outside edge through the middle to the other edge of the pattern, following the pattern line.

- Make four cuts from the outside edge toward the middle of the pattern, following pattern lines.

- Separate the pieces numbered 1 through 6, alternating pieces to make two pie segment design laminations.

- Glue six pieces of wood in a pie segment design on the gluing jig.

- Cut and glue up the remaining wood for the six pie segment laminations.

- Use a belt sander to sand the six pie segment laminations flat and smooth.

- Adhere a pattern to each of the five pie segment laminations, using a pin to center the patterns.

- Cut the outside edge of the patterns for the five pie segment laminations.

MAKING BOXES WITH BOX JOINTS

Box joints are an old technique of joining box sides together. These joints have been cut by hand, table saw, band saw, router, and even on the scroll saw. With a little practice, box joints are easy to cut on your scroll saw. There is very little wasted wood when making a box using box joints, so you can use more expensive woods.

All of the boxes in this chapter are made using box joints. The box bottoms are simply glued onto the box sides.

Two of the boxes use wooden hinges that are designed to hold the lid in an open position. Wooden dowels are used for the hinge pins.

As with anything new, I recommend that you use some scrap wood to practice making hinges and box joints before trying it on the good wood for your box.

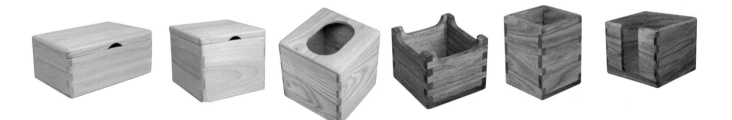

KNITTING BOX

This box is great for storing those small items used in knitting projects. Made from poplar, the box uses wooden hinges that you make on your scroll saw.

Overall size: 6½" long x 2¾" high x 5" deep
Wood: Poplar

TOOLS AND MATERIALS

◆ Two photocopies of the box sides patterns and one photocopy of the lid and lid edge pattern
◆ Two hinges (see pages 92– 93)
◆ #5 reverse-tooth blade for cutting box, lid, and edge
◆ Temporary bond spray adhesive
◆ Gluing jig (see page 3)
◆ Newspaper, to protect gluing jig surface
◆ Wood glue and toothpick
◆ Rag, to wipe away excess glue
◆ Belt sander (optional)
◆ Pencil and square
◆ Sharp blade
◆ Clamps
◆ Clear packaging tape
◆ Sandpaper, 80, 150, and 220 grit
◆ Felt or velvet (optional, for lining)
◆ Finish of choice

STOCK

◆ Two pieces ¼" x 2" x 4½" for box
◆ Two pieces ¼" x 2" x 6½" for box
◆ One piece ¼" x 4" x 6" for lid
◆ Two pieces ¼" x ½" x 4¼" for lid edges A and C
◆ Two pieces ¼" x ½" x 6¾" for lid edges B and D
◆ One piece ¼" x 4¾" x 6¾" for box bottom

Box sides patterns

Make two photocopies
of each pattern.

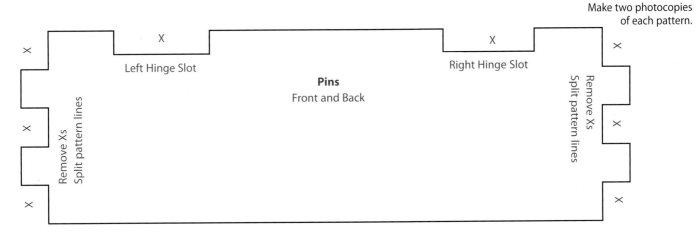

X

Left Hinge Slot

Right Hinge Slot

X

Pins

Front and Back

Remove Xs
Split pattern lines

Remove Xs
Split pattern lines

X

X

X

X

X

X

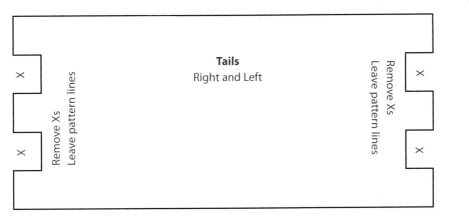

Tails

Right and Left

Remove Xs
Leave pattern lines

Remove Xs
Leave pattern lines

X

X

X

X

QUICK CUTS

BOX

◆ Adhere box sides patterns to stock.

◆ Cut out left and right hinge slots.

◆ Cut out *X*s on box sides.

◆ Glue up box sides.

LID

◆ Glue lid edge B and lid edge D to lid.

◆ Trim lid edge B and lid edge D flush with lid.

◆ Adhere lid edge A pattern to stock.

◆ Cut out *X*s for right and left hinge slots.

◆ Adhere lid edge C pattern to stock.

◆ Cut out *X* for finger lift slot.

◆ Glue lid edge A and lid edge C to lid.

◆ Glue box bottom to box sides.

◆ Glue hinges onto box and lid.

Lid and lid edge pattern

Make one photocopy of the
lid and lid edge pattern.

Enlarge pattern 110%

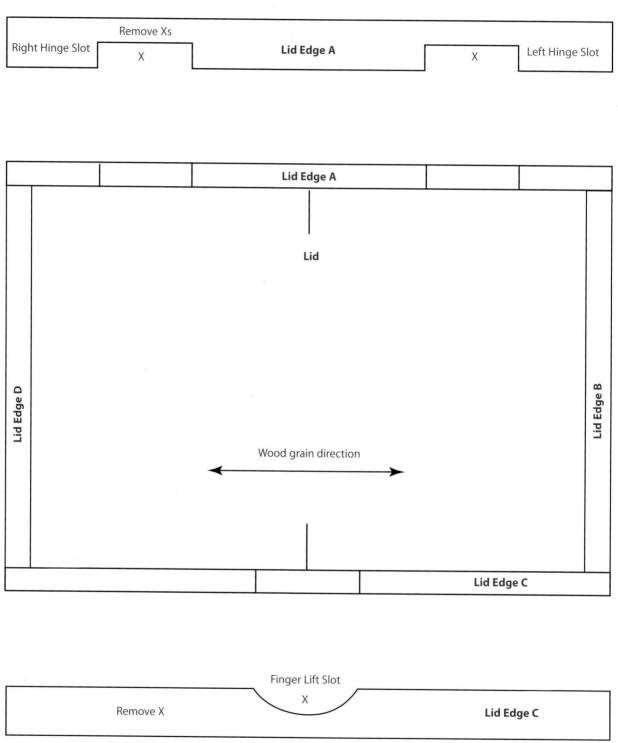

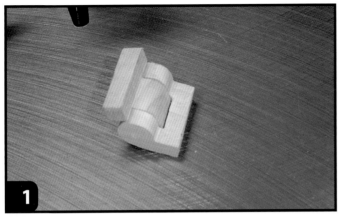

Make two wooden hinges using the instructions on pages 92 and 93.

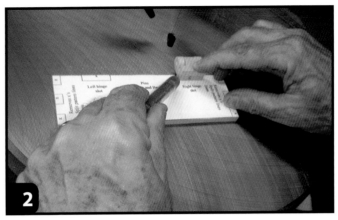

Adhere the box sides patterns to the four box sides. Take one of the pins sides and place one of the hinges on the right hinge slot with the double hinge barrels down. Next, use a sharp blade to make a small cut on both sides of the hinge. You will use these cuts to accurately cut out the hinge slots. Mark the hinge with an *R*. Then, use the other hinge to make cuts on the left hinge slot and mark that hinge with an *L*.

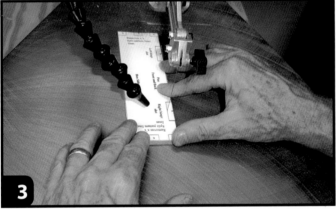

Cut the right hinge slot to the pattern line, keeping your blade between the *X* and your blade cuts. Next, make a 90-degree turn at the hinge slot bottom and cut along the pattern line. Try your R hinge for fit and widen the slot if necessary on the scroll saw. Cut the left hinge slot and test fit the L hinge. The other pins pattern will be the box front and will not have hinge slots.

Cut out the *X*s on the four box sides. Do not cut any hinge slot *X*s on the pins pattern. Make two cuts on the sides of the *X*; Then, make a 90-degree turn and cut along the pattern line to finish the cut. Follow pins and tails instructions on splitting and leaving pattern lines.

Remove the patterns. Dry fit all four sides. If any joints don't fit all the way, widen those joints slightly on the scroll saw. Make sure the side with hinge slots is in back with L at the left and R at the right, as shown in the photo.

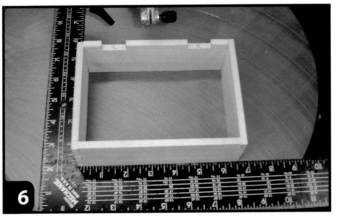

Puddle a small amount of wood glue on a piece of paper. Then, use a toothpick to spread glue in all box joints. Next, glue the four sides together against a square. Check to ensure that the box is glued square. Then, clean up the glue squeeze-out inside the box.

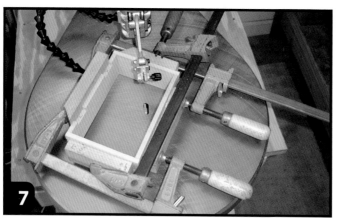

7

Use clamps and scrap wood clamping blocks to clamp the sides together. Let the glue dry.

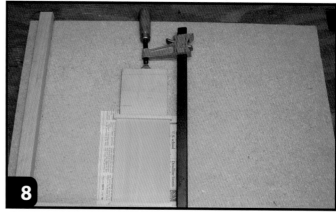

8

Make a gluing jig using the instructions in Chapter One, "Box-Making Basics," on page 3. Glue lid edges B and D onto the lid, letting the lid edges overhang the lid. Check the wood grain direction. Then, clamp the lid edges onto the lid. Clean up the glue squeeze-out and leave clamped for two hours.

9

Cut lid edges B and D flush with the lid.

10

Use a belt sander to sand lid edges B and D flush with the lid.

11

Adhere the lid edge A pattern to a lid edge stock piece of wood. Next, use a sharp blade to mark where hinges L and R fit into the right and left hinge slots with the single hinge barrel. Cut out both hinge slots and dry test fit both hinges. Then, use a pencil to mark the right and left hinge slots. Remove the pattern.

12

Adhere the lid edge C pattern to a lid edge stock piece of wood. Cut out the X, and remove the pattern.

13

Measure and mark a line half the distance between lid edges B and D on both ends of the lid. On lid edge A, mark a line half the distance between the right and left hinge slots. On lid edge C, mark a line half the distance of the finger lift slot width. Use the gluing jig to glue and clamp lid edges A and C onto the lid, following the lines to align the pieces.

14

Put a layer of glue on the four box edges opposite the hinge slots. Place the glued surface on the box bottom piece of wood so that there is approximately ⅛" overhang on the four sides. Clamp the box bottom to the box sides.

15

Cut off the overhanging lid edges. Sand the box and lid on the belt sander. You will be sanding the box bottom flush with the box sides at this point. Then, sand off the pencil marks on the inside of the lid.

16

Glue the hinges into the box and lid hinge slots. Then, apply the finish of your choice.

5

MAKING WOODEN HINGES

TOOLS AND MATERIALS

- Two photocopies of the hinge pattern
- #5 reverse-tooth blade for cutting hinge
- #9 reverse-tooth blade for cutting hinge
- Glue stick
- Drill or drill press and ⅛" and ⁹⁄₆₄" drill bits
- Nail to test fit hinge
- Sandpaper, 220 grit
- Wood glue

STOCK

- One piece ¾" x 1" x 5" hinge blank for two hinges
- One piece ⅛" x 2½" wooden dowel for two hinges

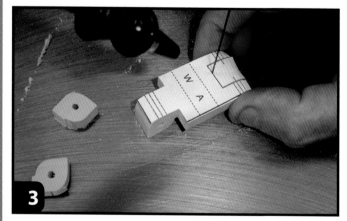

Use a glue stick to adhere the right view hinge patterns to the hinge blank. Drill two ⅛"-diameter holes all the way through the hinge blank as marked on the patterns.

Use a #9 reverse-tooth blade to cut out the profile of the hinge on the scroll saw.

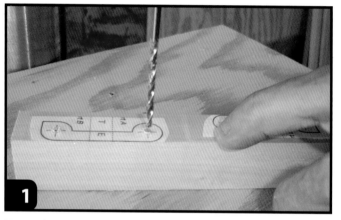

Adhere the top view pattern to the hinge blank. Use a #5 reverse-tooth blade to cut out the hinge barrels along the pattern lines.

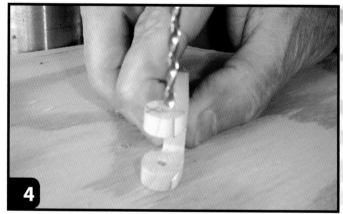

Mark one of the two hinge barrels on side A with an X. Use a ⁹⁄₆₄"-diameter drill bit to enlarge the hinge-pin hole on that side only. Do not enlarge the hinge-pin hole in the other hinge barrel on side A. Enlarge the hinge-pin hole in side B.

MAKING WOODEN HINGES

5

Use a #5 reverse-tooth blade to separate the hinge halves, following pattern lines.

6

Dry assemble the hinge, using the hinge assembly diagram as a guide. Use a nail that fits loosely through the holes to check that the hinge opens freely and doesn't catch or bind at any point.

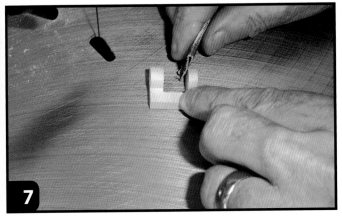

7

Mark any places where the hinges bind. Sand those areas until the hinge opens freely. Then, sand any wood fuzzies off the hinge halves.

8

Assemble the hinges using a ⅛" wooden dowel, referring to the assembly diagram. Insert the dowel through the hinge barrel marked with an *X*, and glue the dowel in place using wood glue. Trim off any overhanging dowel with the scroll saw and sand the area smooth.

9

The assembled hinge.

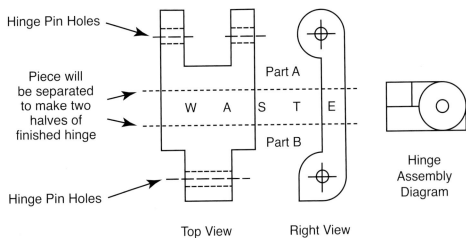

Hinge Pattern Make two photocopies of the hinge pattern.

Hinge Pin Holes

Piece will be separated to make two halves of finished hinge

W A S T E

Part A

Part B

Hinge Pin Holes

Top View

Right View

Hinge Assembly Diagram

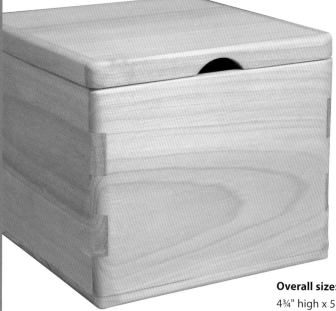

RECIPE BOX

This box is sized to hold and store recipe cards and will make an easy project for your kitchen. I used basswood to make the box, and the wooden hinges hold the lid open, allowing you to hold a recipe card on the inside of the lid.

TOOLS AND MATERIALS

- Two photocopies of the box sides patterns and one photocopy of the lid and lid edge pattern
- Two hinges (see pages 92-93)
- #5 reverse-tooth blade for cutting box, lid, and edge
- Temporary bond spray adhesive
- Gluing jig (see page 3)
- Newspaper, to protect gluing jig surface
- Wood glue and toothpick
- Rag, to wipe away excess glue
- Belt sander (optional)
- Pencil and square
- Sharp blade
- Clamps
- Clear packaging tape
- Sandpaper, 80, 150, and 220 grit
- Felt or velvet (optional, for lining)
- Finish of choice

STOCK

- Four pieces ¼" x 4" x 5¾" for box sides
- One piece ¼" x 5¼" x 5¼" for lid
- Two pieces ¼" x ½" x 6" for lid edges A and C
- Two pieces ¼" x ½" x 5½" for lid edges B and D
- One piece ¼" x 6" x 6" for box bottom

Overall size: 5¾" long x 4¾" high x 5¾" deep
Wood: Basswood

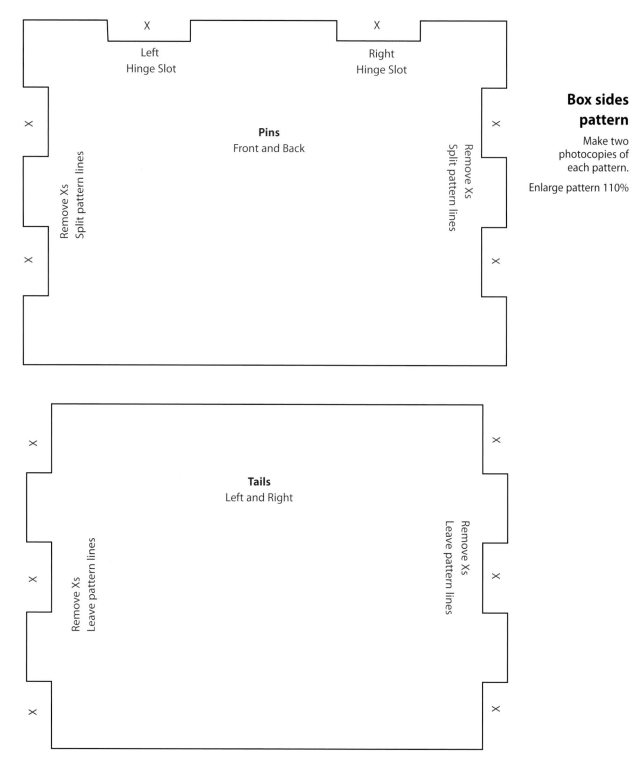

Box sides pattern

Make two photocopies of each pattern.

Enlarge pattern 110%

X X
Left Hinge Slot   Right Hinge Slot

Pins
Front and Back

Remove Xs
Split pattern lines

Remove Xs
Split pattern lines

Tails
Left and Right

Remove Xs
Leave pattern lines

Remove Xs
Leave pattern lines

QUICK CUTS

BOX
◆ Adhere box sides patterns to stock.
◆ Cut out left and right hinge slots.
◆ Cut out *X*s on box sides.
◆ Glue up box sides.

LID
◆ Glue lid edge B and lid edge D to lid.
◆ Trim lid edge B and lid edge D flush with lid.
◆ Adhere lid edge A pattern to stock
◆ Cut out *X*s for right and left hinge slots.

◆ Adhere lid edge C pattern to stock.
◆ Cut out *X* for finger lift slot.
◆ Glue lid edge A and lid edge C to lid.
◆ Glue box bottom to box sides.
◆ Glue hinges onto box and lid.

RECIPE BOX

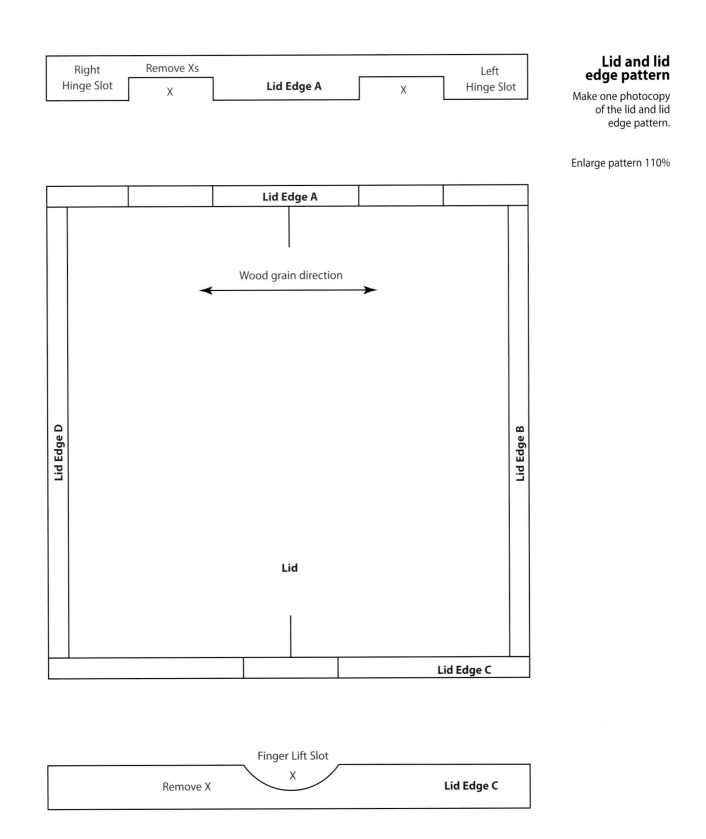

Lid and lid edge pattern

Make one photocopy of the lid and lid edge pattern.

Enlarge pattern 110%

Right Hinge Slot

Remove Xs

X

Lid Edge A

X

Left Hinge Slot

Lid Edge A

Wood grain direction

Lid Edge D

Lid Edge B

Lid

Lid Edge C

Finger Lift Slot

X

Remove X

Lid Edge C

TISSUE BOX COVER

The tissue box cover fits over a standard tissue box and will be a good project to make for the bathroom. I used ash to make this box, which is easy to cut on your scroll saw.

Overall size: 5½" long x 5½" high x 5½" deep
Wood: Ash

TOOLS AND MATERIALS

◆ Two photocopies of the box sides patterns and one photocopy of the lid and lid edge pattern

◆ #5 reverse-tooth blade for cutting box, lid, and edges

◆ Temporary bond spray adhesive

◆ Drill or drill press and ⅟₁₆" drill bit

◆ Gluing jig (see page 3)

◆ Newspaper, to protect gluing jig surface

◆ Wood glue and toothpick

◆ Rag, to wipe away excess glue

◆ Belt sander (optional)

◆ Pencil and square

◆ Clamps

◆ Clear packaging tape

◆ Sandpaper, 80, 150, and 220 grit

◆ Felt or velvet (optional, for lining)

◆ Finish of choice

STOCK

◆ Four pieces ¼" x 5¼" x 5½" for box sides

◆ One piece ¼" x 5¾" x 5¾" for box top

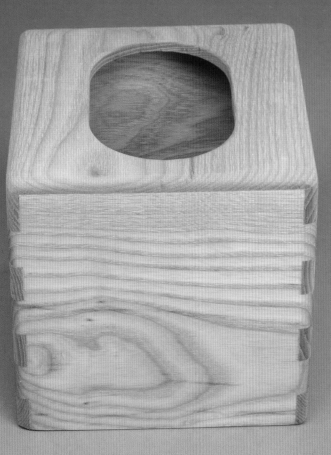

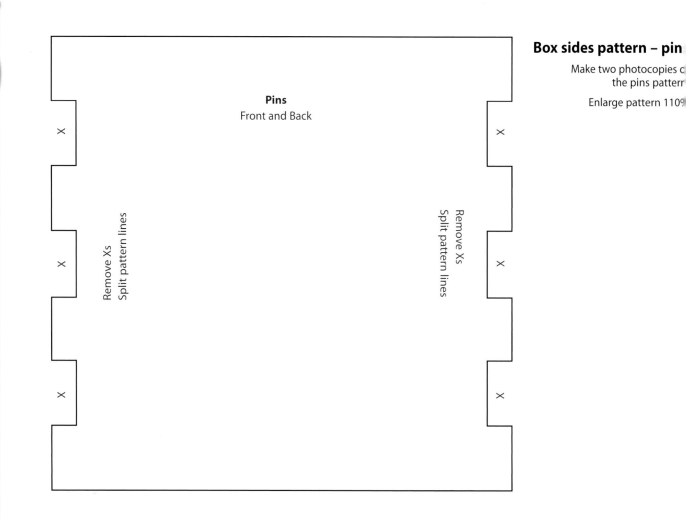

Box sides pattern – pin

Make two photocopies
the pins patterr

Enlarge pattern 110%

Pins
Front and Back

Remove Xs
Split pattern lines

Remove Xs
Split pattern lines

QUICK CUTS

BOX

- Adhere box sides patterns to stock for box.
- Cut out waste area Xs.
- Glue box sides together.

TOP

- Adhere box top pattern to stock for box top.
- Drill 1⁄16" blade entry hole.
- Cut out oval.
- Glue box top to sides.

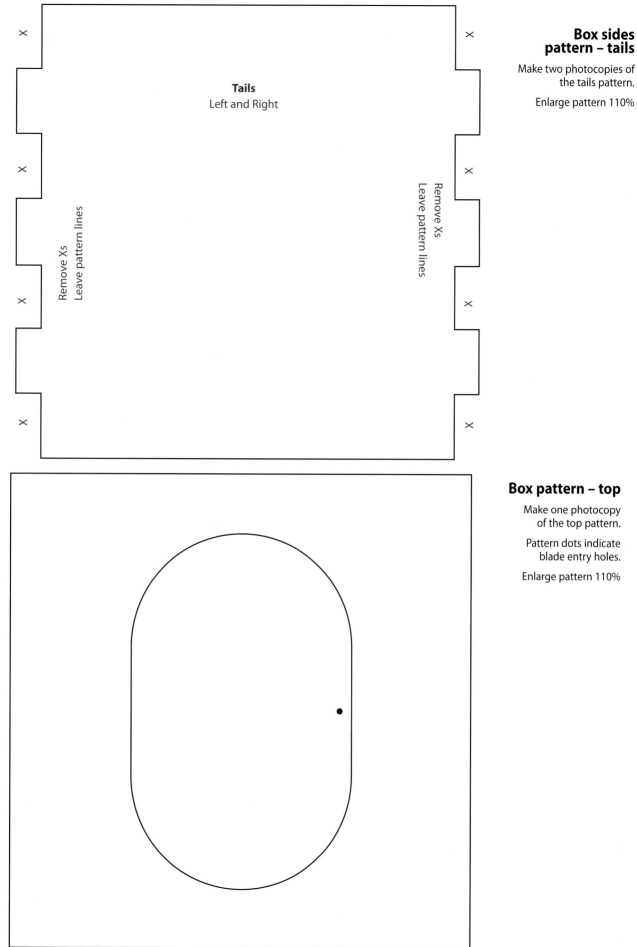

Tails
Left and Right

Remove Xs
Leave pattern lines

Remove Xs
Leave pattern lines

Box sides pattern – tails

Make two photocopies of the tails pattern.

Enlarge pattern 110%

Box pattern – top

Make one photocopy of the top pattern.

Pattern dots indicate blade entry holes.

Enlarge pattern 110%

PAPER CLIP BOX

Your office at home or work probably needs a paper clip box, which is a very small project that you can make on your scroll saw. This box is made from butternut.

Overall size: 3" long x 2½" high x 3" deep
Wood: Butternut

TOOLS AND MATERIALS

◆ Two photocopies of the box sides patterns
◆ #5 reverse-tooth blade for cutting box
◆ Temporary bond spray adhesive
◆ Gluing jig (see page 3)
◆ Newspaper, to protect gluing jig surface
◆ Wood glue and toothpick
◆ Rag, to wipe away excess glue
◆ Belt sander (optional)
◆ Pencil and square
◆ Clamps
◆ Clear packaging tape
◆ Sandpaper, 80, 150, and 220 grit
◆ Felt or velvet (optional, for lining)
◆ Finish of choice

STOCK

◆ Four pieces ¼" x 3" x 2⅛" for box
◆ One piece ¼" x 3⅛" x 3⅛" for box bottom

Box sides patterns

Make two photocopies
of each pattern.

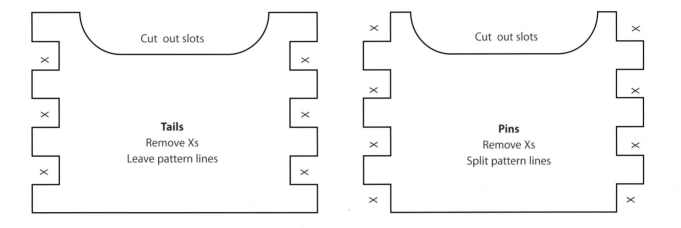

Cut out slots

Tails
Remove Xs
Leave pattern lines

Cut out slots

Pins
Remove Xs
Split pattern lines

QUICK CUTS

- Adhere box sides pattern to stock for box.
- Cut out slots on four sides.
- Cut out *Xs*.
- Glue box sides together.
- Glue box bottom onto sides.

PENCIL AND PEN BOX

This pencil and pen box can be used anywhere that you have pencils and pens or other small office-type items. This box is made from butternut.

Overall size: 3" long x 3¾" high x 3" deep
Wood: Butternut

TOOLS AND MATERIALS

◆ Two photocopies of the box sides patterns
◆ #5 reverse-tooth blade for cutting box
◆ Temporary bond spray adhesive
◆ Gluing jig (see page 3)
◆ Newspaper, to protect gluing jig surface
◆ Wood glue
◆ Toothpick
◆ Rag, to wipe away excess glue
◆ Belt sander (optional)
◆ Pencil and square
◆ Clamps
◆ Clear packaging tape
◆ Sandpaper, 80, 150, and 220 grit
◆ Felt or velvet (optional, for lining)
◆ Finish of choice

STOCK

◆ Four pieces ¼" x 3" x 3½" for box
◆ One piece ¼" x 3⅛" x 3⅛" for box bottom

PENCIL AND PEN BOX

Box sides patterns

Make two photocopies
of each pattern.

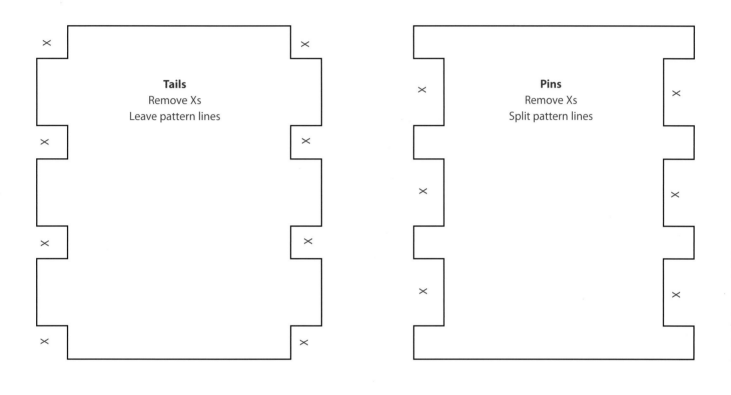

Tails
Remove Xs
Leave pattern lines

Pins
Remove Xs
Split pattern lines

QUICK CUTS

◆ Adhere box sides pattern to stock for box.
◆ Cut out *X*s.
◆ Glue box sides together.
◆ Glue box bottom onto sides.

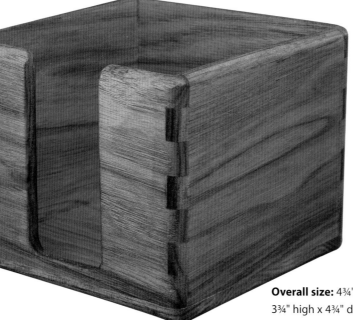

NOTEPAD BOX

Standard-size notepads will fit inside this box that will find a place in your home or office. Butternut was used to make this box.

Overall size: 4¾" long x 3¾" high x 4¾" deep
Wood: Butternut

TOOLS AND MATERIALS

- ◆ Two photocopies of the box sides patterns
- ◆ #5 reverse-tooth blade for cutting box
- ◆ Temporary bond spray adhesive
- ◆ Gluing jig (see page 3)
- ◆ Newspaper, to protect gluing jig surface
- ◆ Wood glue and toothpick
- ◆ Rag, to wipe away excess glue
- ◆ Belt sander (optional)
- ◆ Pencil and square
- ◆ Clamps
- ◆ Clear packaging tape
- ◆ Sandpaper, 80, 150, and 220 grit
- ◆ Felt or velvet (optional, for lining)
- ◆ Finish of choice

STOCK

- ◆ Four pieces ¼" x 3½" x 4¹³⁄₁₆" for box
- ◆ One piece ¼" x 5" x 5" for box bottom

Box sides patterns

Make two photocopies
of each pattern.

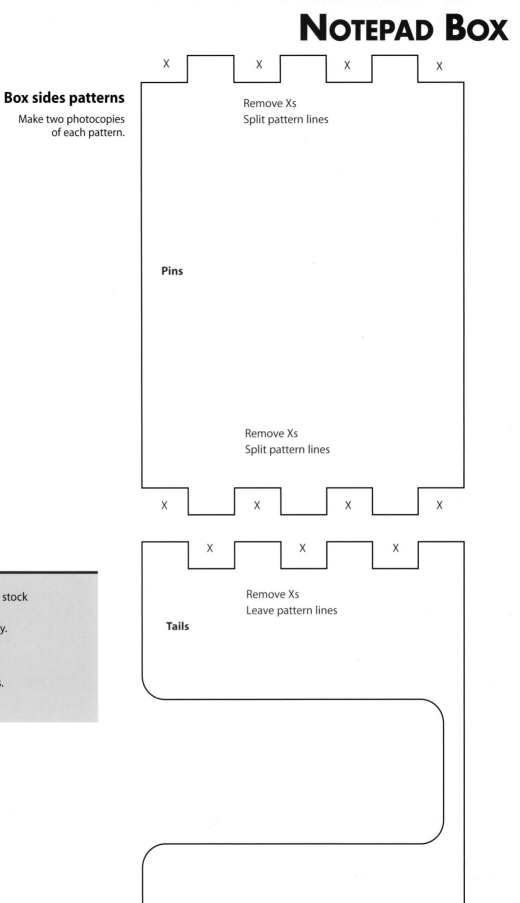

X X X X

Remove Xs
Split pattern lines

Pins

Remove Xs
Split pattern lines

X X X X

X X X

Remove Xs
Leave pattern lines

Tails

Remove Xs
Leave pattern lines

X X X

QUICK CUTS

- Adhere box sides pattern to stock for box.
- Cut out slot on one side only.
- Cut out *X*s.
- Glue box sides together.
- Glue box bottom onto sides.

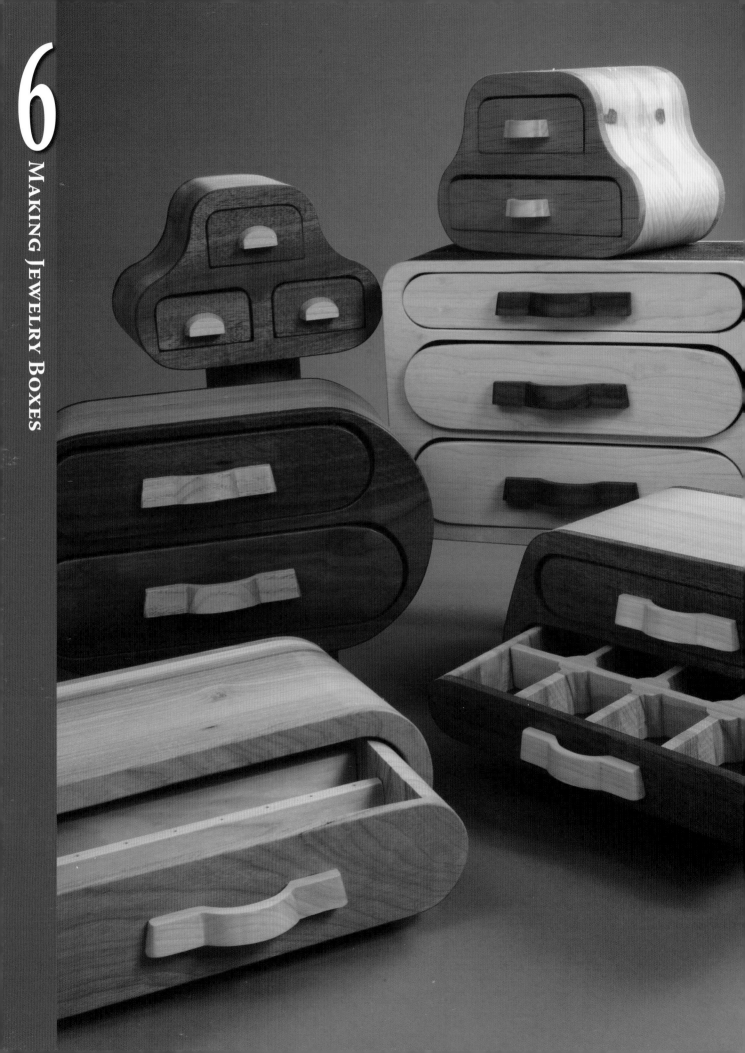

MAKING JEWELRY BOXES

These small, medium, and large boxes are designed to hold jewelry and include compartments, dividers, ring trays, and pierced earring holders. The boxes with compartments, dividers, and ring trays can be easily lined in felt.

The dividers for the drawers are made from the waste wood that you cut out when making the drawers. Ring trays can be made from four pieces of ¾"-thick wood and are designed to be lined in felt that you can easily buy at craft supply stores. Pierced earring holders are made by gluing up

¼"-thick wood and drilling ¹⁄₁₆"-diameter holes to hold the earrings. There are several designs for drawer pulls that can be cut on your scroll saw; select the ones you want from the drawer pulls patterns on page 114.

The step-by-step instructions for the *Jewelry Chest* on pages 110–118 show how to make jewelry boxes with compartments, dividers, ring trays, and pierced earring holders. These boxes will show off your skills using the scroll saw.

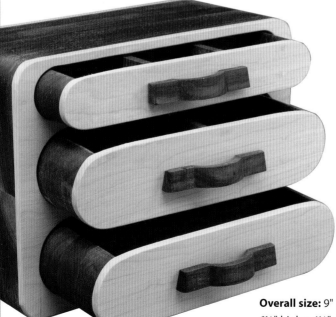

JEWELRY CHEST

This jewelry chest is made for holding jewelry in a medium-sized box. The box is made from maple and walnut, with fancy walnut drawer pulls made on a scroll saw.

Overall size: 9" long x 6½" high x 4¼" deep
Wood: Maple and walnut

TOOLS AND MATERIALS

◆ Seven photocopies of the box pattern
◆ One photocopy each of the ring tray, pierced earring holder, and drawer divider patterns
◆ #5 reverse-tooth blade for box front and back and drawer
◆ #9 reverse-tooth blade for ring tray, box, and drawers
◆ Temporary bond spray adhesive and glue stick
◆ Gluing jig (see page 3)
◆ Newspaper, to protect gluing jig surface
◆ Drill or drill press and ¹⁄₁₆"-diameter drill bit
◆ Wood glue and rag to wipe away excess glue
◆ Drum sander or sandpaper wrapped around wooden dow
◆ Clamps
◆ Double-sided tape
◆ Clear packaging tape
◆ Sandpaper, 80, 150, and 220 grit
◆ Felt or velvet (optional, for lining)
◆ Finish of choice

STOCK

◆ Three pieces ¼" x 1¼" x 6½" for earring holder
◆ Two pieces ¼" x ⅜" x 6½" for earring holder
◆ Two pieces ¼" x 1" x 6½" for earring holder
◆ Four pieces ¾" x 1¼" x 3¾" for ring tray
◆ Five pieces ¾" x 6½" x 9" for jewelry chest
◆ One piece ½" x 6½" x 9" for drawers
◆ Three pieces ¼" x 6½" x 9" for box and drawer fronts and b
◆ ⅜" and ½" stock, depending on drawer pull size

JEWELRY CHEST

Box pattern

Make seven photocopies of the box pattern.

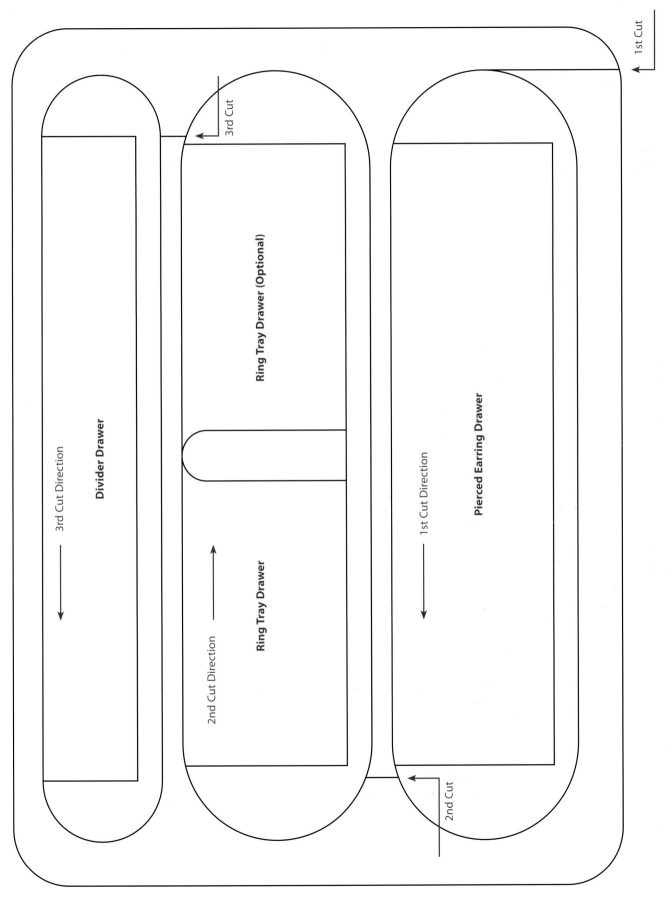

1st Cut

3rd Cut

Ring Tray Drawer (Optional)

Divider Drawer

3rd Cut Direction

Pierced Earring Drawer

1st Cut Direction

Ring Tray Drawer

2nd Cut Direction

2nd Cut

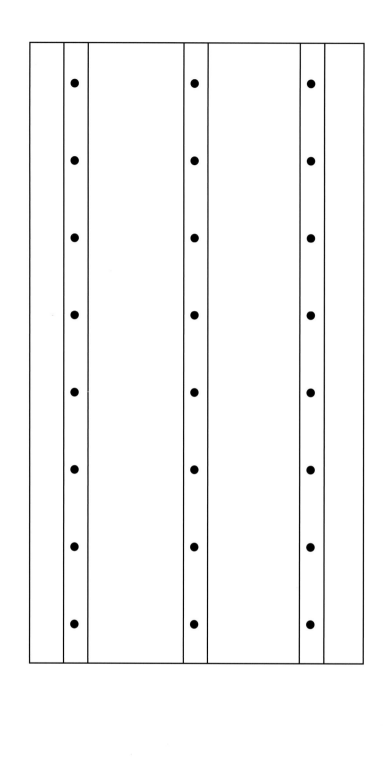

Pierced earring holder pattern

Make one photocopy of the pierced earring holder pattern.

Pattern dots indicate earring holes.

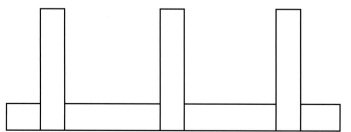

Drawer divider pattern

Make one photocopy of the drawer divider pattern.

Apply pattern to stock and cut out six compartments.

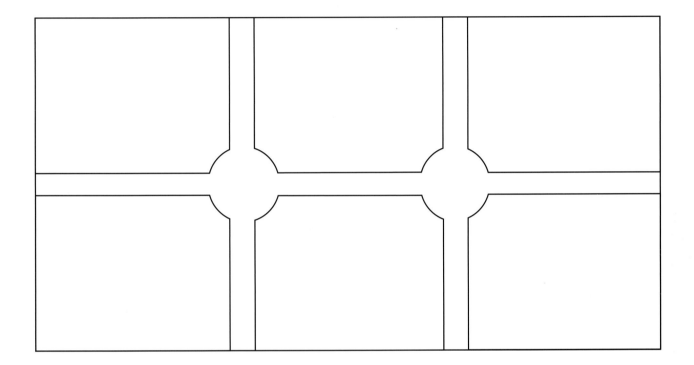

Ring tray pattern

Make one photocopy of the ring tray pattern.

Note: The waste pieces from the pierced earring drawer make one ring tray.

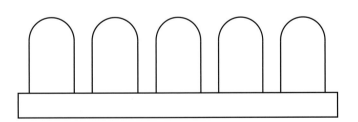

Drawer pulls pattern

Make photocopies to match number of drawer pulls needed.

Enlarge pattern 110%

QUICK CUTS

BOX

- Apply five patterns to five ¾" x 6½" x 9" stock pieces and cut out drawers.
- Glue five ¾" layers together for box.
- Adhere two pieces ¼" x 6½" x 9" stock and cut box profile.
- Separate stack and add last ¼" x 6½" x 9" piece to stack with pattern.
- Cut out the three drawers from the last pieces of ¼" x 6½" x 9" stock.
- Glue box front and back to box.
- Apply one pattern to ½" stock and cut out drawers.
- Glue four ¾"-thick layers and one ½"-thick layer together for drawers.

- Glue drawer fronts and backs to drawers.
- Create divider blank, adhere pattern, and cut out compartments.
- Adhere ring tray patterns to four pieces ¾" x 1¼" x 3⅜" stock and cut out patterns.
- Glue ring tray layers together.
- Apply felt to ring tray holder.
- Glue together earring holder and drill holes marker on pattern.

DRAWER PULLS

- Apply pattern to stock for number of drawer pulls needed.
- Tilt scroll saw table 10 degrees, right side down.
- Cut out drawer pulls, following cut direction arrows.

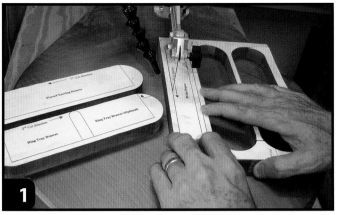

Adhere a pattern to each of the five ¾" x 6½" x 9" stock pieces for the box and drawers. Cover the patterns with clear tape for all five pieces. Next, cut out the pieced earring drawer using a #9 reverse-tooth blade, following the first cut line. Cut out the ring tray drawer, following the second cut line. Then, cut out the divider drawer, following the third cut line.

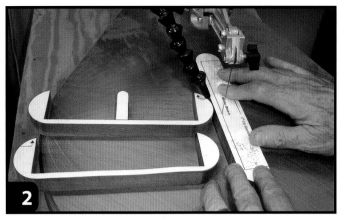

Cut out the compartments for the divider drawer, pierced earring drawer, and ring tray drawer. Save the cut-out waste pieces from the divider drawer and pieced earring holder.

Apply glue to the three saw blade kerfs where the drawers were cut out. Use three clamps to clamp the saw blade kerfs closed. Then, clean up the glue squeeze-out and leave clamped for two hours. Cut out the drawers and compartments from the four remaining pieces, and glue and clamp the saw kerfs closed.

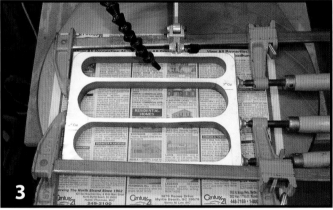

Cut the radius corners or outside profile on the five box layers and remove the patterns.

Glue and clamp three box layers together, clean up glue squeeze-out, and leave them clamped for two hours. Then, glue and clamp the remaining two box layers together, clean up glue squeeze-out, and leave them clamped for two hours.

Use a drum sander or sandpaper wrapped around a dowel to sand the drawer openings on both the two and three box layer pieces of wood.

7

Glue the two and three box layer pieces of wood together. Clamp, clean up glue squeeze-out, and let the glue dry.

8

Use a drum sander to sand the drawer openings on the box. Then, use several strips of double-sided tape to adhere two ¼" x 6½" x 9" box front and back pieces together.

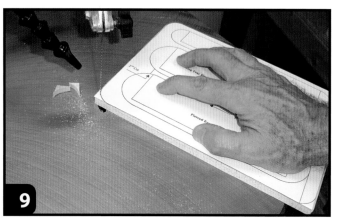

9

Adhere a jewelry chest pattern to the top of the two stacked pieces of wood. Use a #5 reverse-tooth blade to cut off the four corners. Next, separate the two stacked pieces, saving the double-sided tape. Use the tape to adhere the piece with the pattern to the remaining ¼" x 6½" x 9" piece of wood. The piece without the pattern will become the back of the box.

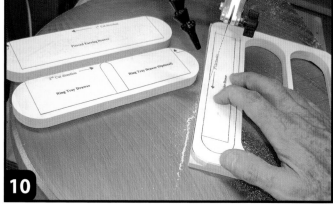

10

Cut out the three drawers, following the first cut, second cut, and third cut directions, from the two stacked pieces. Separate the stacked pieces and remove the pattern. On one piece, glue and clamp the three saw blade kerfs closed. This will become the box front. Discard the other piece—we will only be using the cutouts for the fronts and backs of the drawers.

11

Glue and clamp the front and back pieces onto the box. Clean up glue squeeze-out.

12

Adhere a box pattern to the ½" x 6½" x 9" piece of wood for the drawers. Cut out the three drawers, and then cut out the drawer compartments. Save the divider drawer waste piece.

13

Remove the patterns from the ½"-thick drawer pieces you just cut, and remove the patterns from all ¾"-thick drawer pieces. There are five ¾"-thick drawer pieces for each drawer. Discard one ¾"-thick drawer piece for each drawer. Then, glue and clamp the three drawers together using four ¾"-thick pieces and one ½"-thick piece of wood for each drawer.

14

Sand the compartments on the three drawers.

15

Glue and clamp the drawer fronts and backs onto the three drawers. Clean up the glue squeeze-out.

16

Remove the patterns from the divider drawer waste pieces of wood. Using the gluing jig described in Chapter One, "Box-Making Basics," on page 3, glue and clamp together four ¾"-thick pieces and one ½"-thick piece of wood.

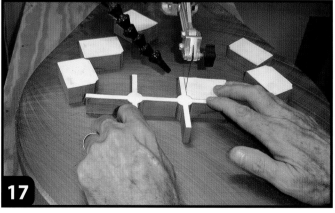

17

Sand the divider blank smooth and ensure that it fits into the divider drawer compartment. Adhere the divider pattern to the divider blank. Cut out the six spaces between the dividers, and then remove the pattern.

18

Adhere the ring tray patterns to the four ¾" x 1¼" x 3⅜" stock for the ring tray. Follow the pattern lines to cut out the ring dividers on the four ¾"-thick layers.

19

Remove the patterns from the ring tray layers. Next, glue and clamp the four ring tray layers together. Then, sand the edges of the ring trays so they fit the compartments.

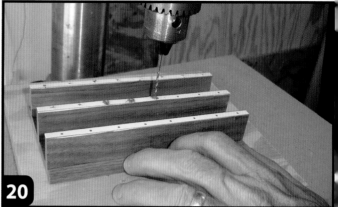

20

Using the gluing jig and the pierced earring holder diagram as reference, glue up the pierced earring holder. Use a glue stick to adhere three hole patterns to the top of the pierced earring holder. Then, drill (24) ¹⁄₁₆"-diameter holes, ½" deep, as indicated on the patterns.

21

Sand the box and drawers smooth, and apply the finish of your choice.

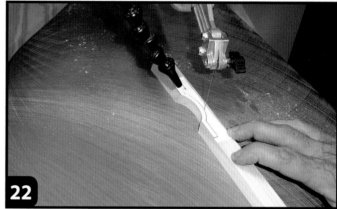

22

Tilt your scroll saw table 10 degrees, right side down. Cut out the drawer pulls in the cut direction shown.

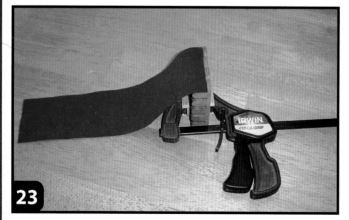

23

To line a ring tray with felt, use a piece of felt that is 3" x 12". Use wood glue to adhere one end of the felt to one end of the ring tray, and leave it glued for one hour.

24

Starting on the end of the ring tray where the felt is glued to the tray, put glue into the ring tray slots and force the felt into the slots with a knife. Trim the felt at the end of the ring tray, and glue that end of felt to the ring tray.

PIERCED EARRING HOLDER

The drawer on this box is designed to hold pierced earrings, and you could easily expand this box to have more drawers for additional storage. The box is made from poplar with a cherry front and back. The drawer pull is made from poplar.

Overall size: 9" long x 3" high x 4¼" deep

Wood: Cherry and poplar

TOOLS AND MATERIALS

◆ Seven photocopies of the box pattern
◆ One photocopy of the pierced earring holder patte
◆ #5 reverse-tooth blade for box front and back and drawer pull
◆ #9 reverse-tooth blade for pierced earring holder, b and drawer
◆ Temporary bond spray adhesive
◆ Gluing jig (see page 3)
◆ Newspaper, to protect gluing jig surface
◆ Drill or drill press and ¹⁄₁₆"-diameter drill bit
◆ Wood glue and rag to wipe away excess glue
◆ Drum sander or sandpaper wrapped around wooden dowel
◆ Clamps
◆ Double-sided tape
◆ Clear packaging tape
◆ Sandpaper, 80, 150, and 220 grit
◆ Felt or velvet (optional, for lining)
◆ Finish of choice

STOCK

◆ Five pieces ¾" x 3" x 9½" for box and drawer
◆ One piece ½" x 2" x 8¼" for drawer
◆ Three pieces ¼" x 3" x 9½" for box and drawer fron and backs

PIERCED EARRING HOLDER

Box pattern

Make seven photocopies of the pattern.

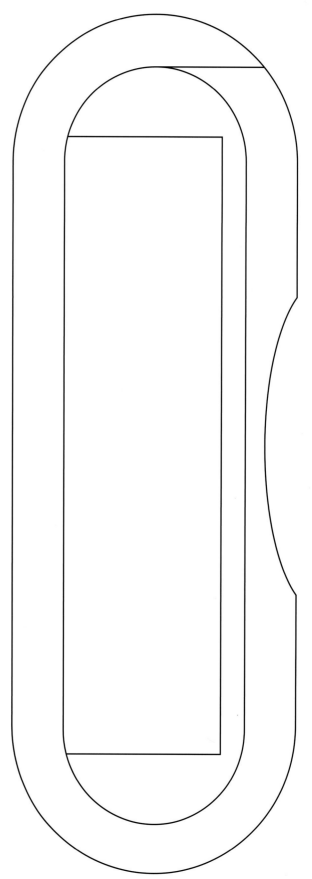

QUICK CUTS

BOX

◆ Apply five patterns to five ¾" x 3" x 9½" stock pieces and cut out drawer.

◆ Glue five ¾" layers together for box.

◆ Adhere two pieces ¼" x 3" x 9½" stock and cut box profile.

◆ Separate stack and add last ¼" x 3" x 9½" piece to stack with pattern.

◆ Cut out drawer from the last pieces of ¼" x 3" x 9½" stock.

◆ Glue box front and back to box.

◆ Apply one top drawer pattern and one bottom drawer pattern to ½" stock and cut out drawers.

◆ Glue four ¾"-thick layers and one ½"-thick layer together for drawer.

◆ Glue drawer front and back to drawer.

◆ Glue together earring holder and drill holes marked on pattern on page 112.

DRAWER PULLS

◆ Apply pattern to stock for number of drawer pulls needed.

◆ Tilt scroll saw table 10 degrees, right side down.

◆ Cut out drawer pulls, following cut direction arrows.

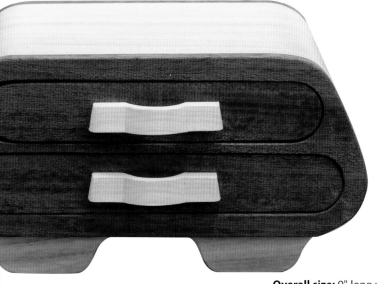

SCROLL SAWN DIVIDERS BOX

This box features compartment dividers in a uniquely shaped box. I used basswood for the box and mahogany for the contrasting box front and back. Basswood was also used for the drawer pulls.

Overall size: 9" long x 4¾" high x 4¼" deep

Wood: Basswood and mahogany

TOOLS AND MATERIALS

- ◆ Seven photocopies of the box pattern
- ◆ Two photocopies of the drawer divider pattern
- ◆ #5 reverse-tooth blade for box front and back and drawer pu
- ◆ #9 reverse-tooth blade for dividers, box, and drawers
- ◆ Temporary bond spray adhesive
- ◆ Gluing jig (see page 3)
- ◆ Newspaper, to protect gluing jig surface
- ◆ Drill or drill press and ¹⁄₁₆"-diameter drill bit
- ◆ Wood glue and rag to wipe away excess glue
- ◆ Drum sander or sandpaper wrapped around wooden dowe
- ◆ Clamps
- ◆ Double-sided tape
- ◆ Clear packaging tape
- ◆ Sandpaper, 80, 150, and 220 grit
- ◆ Felt or velvet (optional, for lining)
- ◆ Finish of choice

STOCK

- ◆ Five pieces ¾" x 5" x 9½" for box and drawers
- ◆ One piece ½" x 1½" x 16" for drawers
- ◆ Waste pieces from cutting out the top and bottom compartments for the dividers
- ◆ Two pieces ¼" x 4¼" x 9½" for front and back of box and fronts of drawers
- ◆ One piece ¼" x 1½" x 16" top and bottom drawer backs

Scroll Sawn Dividers Box

Box pattern

Make seven photocopies of the pattern.

Enlarge pattern 120%

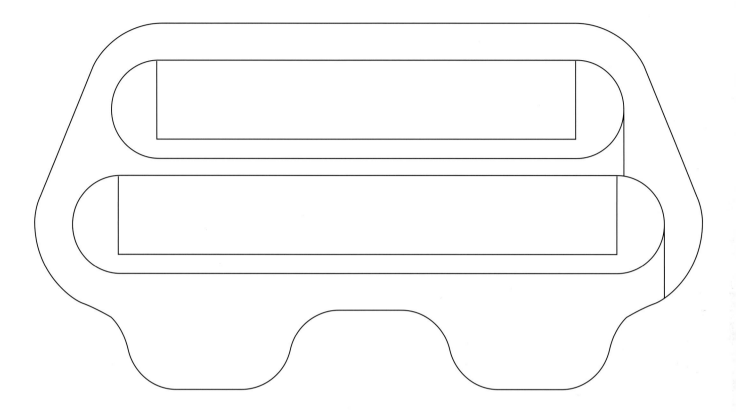

Quick Cuts

Box

- Apply five patterns to five ¾" x 5" x 9½" stock pieces and cut out drawers.
- Glue five ¾" layers together for box.
- Adhere two pieces ¼" x 4¼" x 9½" stock and cut box profile.
- Separate stack and add last ¼" x 4¼" x 9½" piece to stack with pattern.
- Cut out the two drawers from the last pieces of ¼" x 4¼" x 9½" stock.
- Glue box front and back to box.
- Apply one top drawer pattern and one bottom drawer pattern to ½" stock and cut out drawers.
- Glue four ¾"-thick layers and one ½"-thick layer together for drawers.
- Glue drawer fronts and backs to drawers.
- Apply top drawer divider pattern to small divider blank.
- Cut out six divider compartments.
- Apply bottom drawer divider pattern to large divider blank.
- Cut out eight divider compartments.

Drawer Pulls

- Apply pattern to stock for number of drawer pulls needed.
- Tilt scroll saw table 10 degrees, right side down.
- Cut out drawer pulls, following cut direction arrows.

Box pattern
Make one photocopy of the pattern.

SCROLL SAWN DIVIDERS BOX

Dividers

Make one photocopy of the patterns.

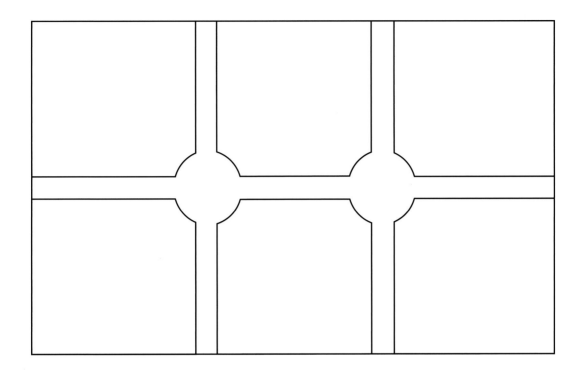

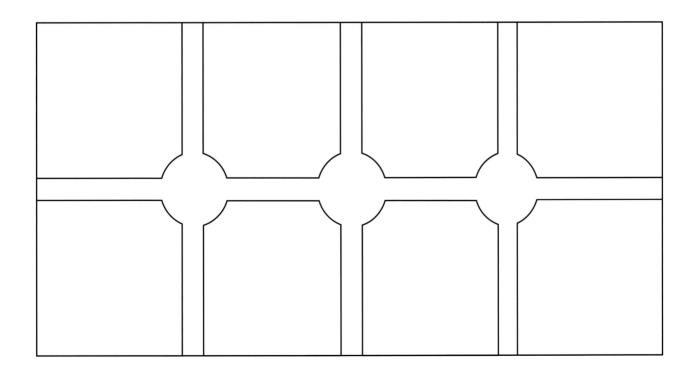

RING TRAY BOX

This box has a ring tray and separate compartments for storing small jewelry items. The box and its drawer pulls are made from sassafras with a contrasting walnut front and back.

Overall size: 9" long x 5" high x 4¼" deep
Wood: Sassafras and walnut

TOOLS AND MATERIALS

- ◆ Seven photocopies of the box pattern
- ◆ Two photocopies of the ring tray pattern (see page 11
- ◆ #5 reverse-tooth blade for box front and back and drawer pulls
- ◆ #9 reverse-tooth blade for ring trays, box, and drawe
- ◆ Glue stick
- ◆ Gluing jig (see page 3)
- ◆ Newspaper, to protect gluing jig surface
- ◆ Drill or drill press and ¹⁄₁₆"-diameter drill bit
- ◆ Wood glue and rag to wipe away excess glue
- ◆ Drum sander or sandpaper wrapped around wooden dowel
- ◆ Clamps
- ◆ Double-sided tape
- ◆ Clear packaging tape
- ◆ Sandpaper, 80, 150, and 220 grit
- ◆ Felt or velvet (optional, for lining)
- ◆ Finish of choice

STOCK

- ◆ Five pieces ¾" x 5" x 9½" for box and drawers
- ◆ One piece ½" x 5" x 9½" for drawers
- ◆ Three pieces ¼" x 5" x 9½" for box and drawer fronts and backs

RING TRAY BOX

Box pattern

Make seven photocopies
of the box pattern.

Enlarge pattern 110%

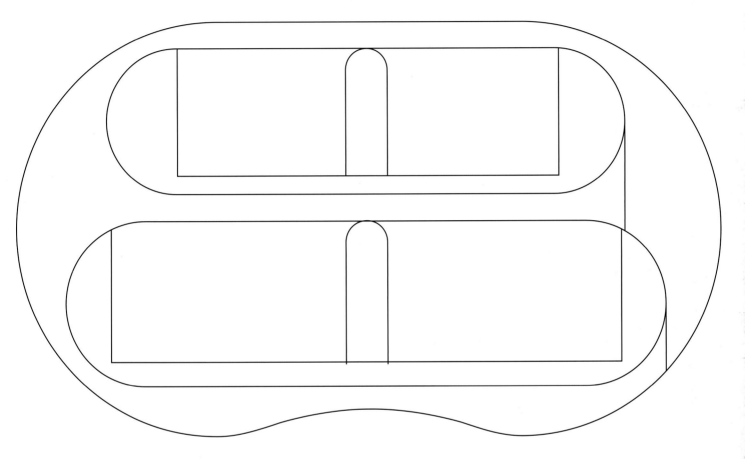

QUICK CUTS

BOX

- Apply five patterns to five ¾" x 5" x 9½" stock pieces and cut out drawers.

- Glue five ¾" layers together for box.

- Adhere two pieces ¼" x 5" x 9½" stock and cut box profile.

- Separate stack and add last ¼" x 5" x 9½" piece to stack with pattern.

- Cut out the two drawers from the last pieces of ¼" x 5" x 9½" stock.

- Glue box front and back to box.

- Apply one pattern to ½" stock and cut out drawers.

- Glue four ¾"-thick layers and one ½"-thick layer together for drawers.

- Glue drawer fronts and backs to drawers.

- Adhere ring tray patterns (see page 113) to four pieces ¾" x 1¼" x 3⅜" stock and cut out patterns.

- Glue ring tray layers together.

- Apply felt to ring tray holder.

DRAWER PULLS

- Apply pattern to stock for number of drawer pulls needed.

- Tilt scroll saw table 10 degrees, right side down.

- Cut out drawer pulls, following cut direction arrows.

SMALL TWO-DRAWER BOX

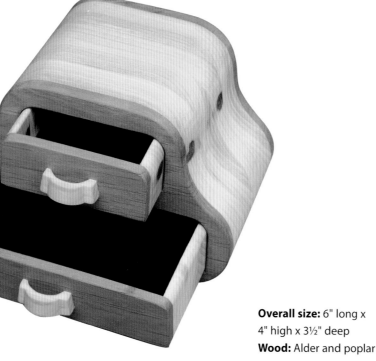

This box makes a great gift for a child as a first jewelry box in a unique, easy-to-make shape. The front and back of the box are made from alder, and the box and drawer pulls are made from poplar.

Overall size: 6" long x 4" high x 3½" deep
Wood: Alder and poplar

TOOLS AND MATERIALS

- Six photocopies of the box pattern
- #5 reverse-tooth blade for box front and back and drawer pulls
- #9 reverse-tooth blade for the box and drawers
- Temporary bond spray adhesive
- Gluing jig (see page 3)
- Newspaper, to protect gluing jig surface
- Drill or drill press and ¹⁄₁₆"-diameter drill bit
- Wood glue and rag to wipe away excess glue
- Drum sander or sandpaper wrapped around wooden dowel
- Clamps
- Double-sided tape
- Clear packaging tape
- Sandpaper, 80, 150, and 220 grit
- Felt or velvet (optional, for lining)
- Finish of choice

STOCK

- Four pieces ¾" x 4" x 6½" for box and drawers
- One piece ½" x 1¼" x 9" for drawers
- Three pieces ¼" x 4" x 6½" for box and drawer fronts and backs

SMALL TWO-DRAWER BOX

Box pattern

Make six photocopies
of the box pattern.

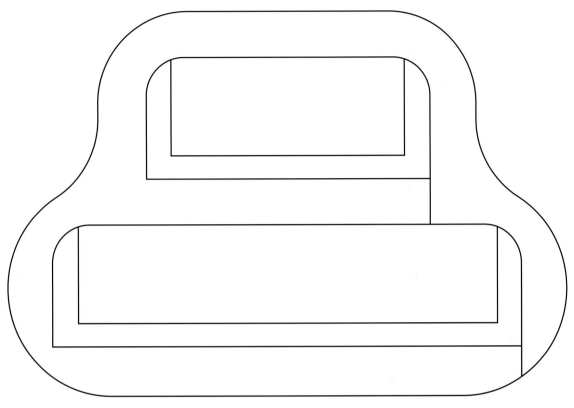

QUICK CUTS

BOX

- Apply four patterns to four ¾" x 4" x 6½" stock pieces and cut out drawers.

- Glue four ¾" layers together for box.

- Adhere two pieces ¼" x 4" x 6½" stock and cut box profile.

- Separate stack and add last ¼" x 4" x 6½" piece to stack with pattern.

- Cut out the two drawers from the last pieces of ¼" x 4" x 6½" stock.

- Glue box front and back to box.

- Apply one top drawer pattern and one bottom drawer pattern to ½" stock and cut out drawers.

- Glue four ¾"-thick layers and one ½"-thick layer together for drawers.

- Glue drawer fronts and backs to drawers.

DRAWER PULLS

- Apply pattern to stock for number of drawer pulls needed.

- Tilt scroll saw table 10 degrees, right side down.

- Cut out drawer pulls, following cut direction arrows.

SMALL THREE-DRAWER BOX

This small box has drawers for storing small jewelry items and makes a great gift for anyone. The box is made from ash with more expensive mahogany for the box front and back. Ash was also used for the drawer pulls.

Overall size: 6" long x 4" high x 3½" deep
Wood: Ash and mahogany

TOOLS AND MATERIALS

- ◆ Six photocopies of the box pattern
- ◆ #5 reverse-tooth blade for box front and back and drawer pulls
- ◆ #9 reverse-tooth blade for the box and drawers
- ◆ Temporary bond spray adhesive
- ◆ Gluing jig (see page 3)
- ◆ Newspaper, to protect gluing jig surface
- ◆ Drill or drill press and ¹⁄₁₆"-diameter drill bit
- ◆ Wood glue and rag to wipe away excess glue
- ◆ Drum sander or sandpaper wrapped around wooden dowel
- ◆ Clamps
- ◆ Double-sided tape
- ◆ Clear packaging tape
- ◆ Sandpaper, 80, 150, and 220 grit
- ◆ Felt or velvet (optional, for lining)
- ◆ Finish of choice

STOCK

- ◆ Four pieces ¾" x 4" x 6½" for box and drawers
- ◆ One piece ½" x 1¼" x 8" for drawers
- ◆ Three pieces ¼" x 4" x 6½" for box and drawer fronts and backs

SMALL THREE-DRAWER BOX

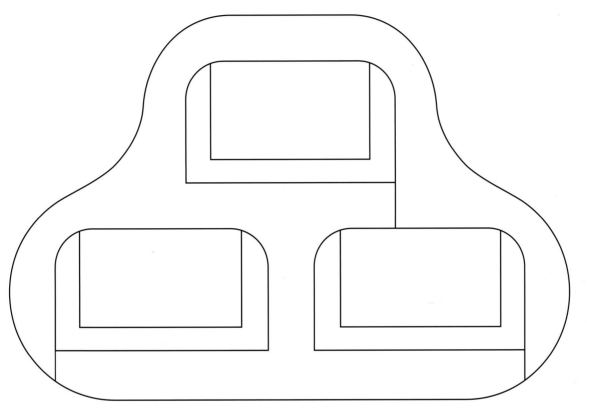

QUICK CUTS

BOX

◆ Apply four patterns to four
¾" x 4" x 6½" stock pieces and
cut out drawers.

◆ Glue four ¾" layers together
for box.

◆ Adhere two pieces ¼" x 4" x 6½"
stock and cut box profile.

◆ Separate stack and add last
¼" x 4" x 6½" piece to stack
with pattern.

◆ Cut out the three drawers
from the last pieces of
¼" x 4" x 6½" stock.

◆ Glue box front and back to box.

◆ Apply one top drawer pattern
and one bottom drawer pattern
to ½" stock and cut out drawers.

◆ Glue four ¾"-thick layers and
one ½"-thick layer together
for drawers.

◆ Glue drawer fronts and
backs to drawers.

DRAWER PULLS

◆ Apply pattern to stock for
number of drawer pulls needed.

◆ Tilt scroll saw table 10 degrees,
right side down.

◆ Cut out drawer pulls, following
cut direction arrows.

Appendix:

Lamination Quick Reference Chart

	Lamination	Stock Sizes	Wood	Laminated Layers
	Checkerboard	12 pieces, ½" x 1" x 13"	6 pieces light colored, 6 pieces dark colored	6 pieces, ½" x 4" x 6½"
	Diamond	12 pieces, ½" x 1" x 15"	6 pieces light colored, 6 pieces dark colored	6 pieces, ½" x 4" x 7½"
	Four Woods	12 pieces, ½" x 1" x 17"	3 pieces each of four different woods	6 pieces, ½" x 4" x 8½"
	Pinwheel	6 pieces, ½" x 5½" x 5½"	3 pieces light colored, 3 pieces dark colored	6 pieces, ½" x 5½" x 5½
	Pie Segment	6 pieces, ½" x 5½" x 5½"	3 pieces light colored, 3 pieces dark colored	6 pieces, ½" x 5½" x 5½

INDEX

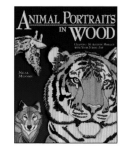